Head♡less Chicken

A Personal Narrative about Three Months in
the Amazon, Ayahuasca, and Old Stories

Manuela Stoerzer

© 2019 by Manuela Stoerzer

All rights reserved. No part of this book, in part or in whole, may be reproduced, transmitted or utilized in any form or by any means, electronic, photographic or mechanical, including photocopying, recording, or by any information storage and retrieval system without permission in writing from Ozark Mountain Publishing, Inc. except for brief quotations embodied in literary articles and reviews.

For permission, serialization, condensation, adaptions, or for our catalog of other publications, write to Ozark Mountain Publishing, Inc., P.O. Box 754, Huntsville, AR 72740, ATTN: Permissions Department.

Library of Congress Cataloging-in-Publication Data

Stoerzer, Manuela – 1965 -
Headless Chicken by Manuela Stoerzer

Be yourself-not your story! This book is an invitation to accompany a journey through the jungle of the mind.

1. Healing 2. Shamanic 3.Spiritual 4. Metaphysical
I. Stoerzer, Manuela, 1965 - II. Metaphysical III. Spiritual IV. Title

Library of Congress Catalog Card Number: 2019940245
ISBN: 9781940265742

Cover Art and Layout: Victoria Cooper Art
Book set in: Viner Hand ITC, Bell MT
Book Design: Tab Pillar
Published by:

PO Box 754, Huntsville, AR 72740
800-935-0045 or 479-738-2348; fax 479-738-2448
WWW.OZARKMT.COM

Printed in the United States of America

Contents

Preface	i
1 - How It All Began	1
2 - The Journey Has Already Started	8
3 - Arriving in Iquitos	12
4 - First Ayahuasca Experience	17
5 - Second Ayahuasca Experience	25
6 - Third Ayahuasca Night	33
7 - New Year's in the Amazon	42
8 - Ayahuasca Trip 4	46
9 - A New Start	49
10 - Ayahuasca Trip 5	60
11 - Two Days Off	67
12 - Cutting Down Resistance	74
13 - Ayahuasca Trip 7	82
14 - Done Healing	92
15 - Ayahuasca Trip 11	97
16 - A Week in Punta Hermosa	114
17 - "Final" Insights	124
18 - Leaving the Retreat Center	150
19 - Time to Move On	155
20 - The Real Magic Starts	160
21 - What Difference Did the Shamanic Work Make?	179
22 - From Now On, What?	188
Epilogue	195
About the Author	197

Preface

Someone once said everyone has to plant a tree, have a child, and write a book. I am not a fan of copying what other people do. In fact, I believe this is the reason for a lot of trouble and misery. We miss being ourselves. We just take on what we have learned from others.

I believe that this is the reason why many people are unhappy. Well, one reason. We take on what our parents did. They did what their parents did, and we miss the whole point: finding out who we really are, what our God-given gift is and what to do with it.

The purpose of this book is to inspire readers to look deeper inside themselves and start asking some important questions beyond or better way before "how will I finance my pension plan." Who are we really beyond the roles and ideas we all took on? What is underneath? Polish your diamond, get to the grits! No need to be proud and no need to be ashamed. Just clear the bulk away, find out and be yourself.

This is my story, how I perceived it subjectively at the time. Please excuse all those "I's." This is about a search and what I found during a spontaneous three-month stay in the Amazon rain forest. I went there to translate Spanish into English, German and French and vice versa and ended up celebrating lots of shamanic Ayahuasca healing plant ceremonies that reminded me about the truth the hard way. Nothing that you need Ayahuasca for, since we all have it inside, but almost forgotten.

I had started writing a book several times. Each time, after around eighty pages, I stopped because my inner critic told me, don't waste other people's time with more insignificant stories. Who wants to read your stuff? There is so much information out there ... Too much information polluting people's minds ... Plus, it is just my subjective view at the time, anyway. Yet, it was important to express something about myself that had not been heard. Deep down, we are all paddling in the same kind of boat in the same ocean. Writing a book, you think of a given form, chapters or a chronological order. Trying to put what I wanted to share into chapters killed the flow. I just couldn't do it. The intention was not to write a chronological biography of a troubled child that finds healing with hallucinogenic drugs and which was not the case anyway. The intention is to share an experienced story that reveals how we create an illusionary reality based on conditioning, copying, secrecies or lies and assumptions. And how we interpret what we experience with our senses in such a way that it would fit to our false idea of reality.

This is an attempt to share from a soul perspective how mind and emotions work and influence and how any situation, problem and trauma can be perceived in different ways and create distortions and false beliefs. And it is also about how this drama can be healed once we realize who we really are. I want to inspire others to question who or what they are, to free themselves from limiting and separating ideas, to surrender to a higher power that we are part of, to find trust, love and joy.

Many people have asked me about the three-month experience in the Peruvian jungle when I came back. They wanted to find out whether Ayahuasca would be the solution to heal from suffering. I don't think so. My humble opinion after the Amazon experience is that prayer, deep meditation or experiences in nature can help transcend suffering just as much. It's about us being conscious, present, compassionate, and responsible to allow love in (crack the nut) and to share that love.

Here, I just share my experiences with Ayahuasca, and what that meant in respect of my life experience and personal background. It is important to point out that other people's experiences are other people's experiences and nothing more. What that means for me is not what it means for you. Everybody has their own perspective, frames of mind, background and path. And yet, we have very similar mechanisms going and we are made of the same stuff. Sometimes, being understanding and compassionate with others can help to apply the same kindness to ourselves.

The initial storyline for this book is a little daily diary that I wrote from the end of December 2014 to April 2015, mostly directly after

Preface

Ayahuasca ceremonies, to remember my experiences under the influence of the shamanic drug. Typing it all down in retrospect two years later, I also expose the personal stories that relate to the insights and messages I got "from" Ayahuasca—personally. I don't believe there is a mother Ayahuasca who talks and reveals to you, but you just transcend ego filters temporarily under the influence. Ayahuasca contains DMT, a psychedelic drug that has historically been prepared by various cultures for ritual and healing purposes.

This is about understanding what cause may influence a symptom and what message wants to be heard, understood and responded to differently in the future. What part of ourselves we have been successfully suppressing, ignoring, or intensively kept hidden in the dark. I am a firm believer in nature's intelligence, I believe in God, I believe nature works in the best possible way. Always. A seed sprouts in the right environment at the right time without knowing how and why. Deep down I know there is some kind of magic and intelligence behind all the things we experience, a higher force we are connected to, part of, made of. Even though there are so many situations that we just cannot understand nor accept with our conditioned mind, years later, we may understand. This book is written to share some of my continuous journey to understanding who I am, how life works and what we are here for. No matter how many Ayahuasca ceremonies or esoteric practices you do, I believe the ego doesn't die. It may be transcended temporarily, it may hide, it may mask itself, it may be kept in check. We do need direction in life. Ayahuasca is not a direction.

Doubting, suffering and standing in your own way can still continue, unless we learn, appreciate and accept that our temporary body is just a vehicle, the intellect is just a tool, and so are feelings, not good, not bad, just guidelines.

Ayahuasca is one out of thousands of ways how ancient shamanic knowledge and natural healing plants were used to help people heal themselves. Today, it is pretty much taken out of context, a business. Experienced shaman healers used to know what remedy to offer to a person looking for help, when they took a small amount of the drug themselves. Some people who suffered from any kind of abuse or depression report amazing healings happening with the plant medicine, and now they think this is the power remedy for everybody. I don't think so. It does help to become more compassionate with yourself, not just know, but feel. See beyond the layers that the ego has created to "protect" from further damage and at the same time keep you trapped in the prison of suppressed old stuff.

Others hope an Ayahuasca trip would be a magic solution for drama and despair. I believe you still need to change the way you do the things you do, every day.

Some think drinking Ayahuasca is like a magic shot that makes you forget everything that has happened in the past, that it will free you from former traumas so you no longer remember what has happened or how you experienced it. Like a complete wipe out. It doesn't work like that.

To see a kind of hallucinogen magic, once habitual thinking is temporarily gone is quite amazing and yet, if you can't make sense of it, it is a lot of hardship to see some sprinkling stars and fairy-tale land or snakes and dark stuff.

Writing this book is a way for me to remember exactly that. Hopefully this narrative may foster hope and courage to also accept, acknowledge and appreciate who you are, the way you are. Realize that what you think you are is just what you think you are, through your filters, and explore in silence again and again that you are so much more. Realize when emotions are triggered and know that they have not much to do with here and now, but with an old unhealed story that wants to be heard and healed.

So what are we if not a piece of flesh with the computer on top? I cannot answer this question for you, because when I tell you what I feel I am, I might deprive you from finding out for yourself and then, the information is nothing but somebody else's (my) opinion. Like reading another book, adding information to the database, without ever really experiencing *and* feeling it. I share my story and my truth for you to discover your own.

This book is kind of writing itself, as if it was already written. No need for structure. I guess you can't undo or realign the truth. No book to read fast. A book to start feeling inside.

1 - How It All Began

Magic Happens

Strolling around Santa Catalina, Mallorca, I bumped into that old friend that I hadn't seen in many years. Thirteen years ago, when I first came to the island, I used to hang out with him every once in a while, go for hikes or do excursions with the kids. We seemed to have a good connection, yet I never wanted to hang out too long with him. We had joint interests and goals about how we can become better people, possibly support people to become healthier. Having a good time together is a good reason to hang out besides inspiring each other. He knew so much about health, yoga, food, vitamins and also about practical things like building, fixing, electricity, you name it. In great shape, healthy, strong, but just had a hard time to be OK in his skin and where he was ... I guess the medical term might be depression. For some reason, he didn't seem to be able to be content, at peace or accepting of what is for long.

A couple of months earlier I had separated from my second husband. Even though I was not proud of the second failed marriage, I was proud of having been (almost) totally honest and leaving a relationship. Almost, because I held back to share some feelings of anger, fear and sadness when separating. He wanted something else than I did. A value issue. Not that I don't like luxury. It is simply not that important to me. We had two different visions and priorities in life. It was not a matter of lack of love but it was a matter of loving myself more than staying with him in order to not hurt him. So he concluded I didn't love him. I couldn't find a way to express myself and gave up hope, to be able to speak my truth until the day I left. I preferred to accept being "the bad guy" for him and probably the people we both knew, despite the inner conflict, just could not find a way to express my own feelings. Today I know the decision to separate was a loving one, also for him, even though he suffered and was hurt. I didn't know why, but I

Headless Chicken

knew that there was no future as a couple for us together. During four years I had attempted to change myself in a way so I would be okay with the situation and fit into his world. And yet, I did not feel at the right time at the right place, nor did I feel I was in the relationship I was supposed to be in for the rest of my life. To be honest, we did not want to get married in the first place. We did feel a deep "spiritual" connection and love and understanding. That's why we had considered to live together and find out what would happen. So I moved to the States and got married, to be able to stay in the US together with him. During that process, I could not leave the country until I got the green card. That first winter was a long one in Lake Tahoe. Six months snow. At that time I did not trust myself, my own feelings. I somehow did not want to accept that what I felt was right. I doubted my own feelings. Ridiculous! Instead of listening to my feelings and acting accordingly, I thought [thought!] there is something wrong with me anyway, and I needed to better myself ... Why I thought that you will find out later on in the book.

So here I am, after another separation, back in Majorca. I had no clue of what I was going to do next. All I knew was, I had to sort out the situation. We tried to live together in Majorca but he did not like it here, nor did he see himself making a living here. I did not like it in Nevada. Nor was I in a position where I could totally surrender myself, even though I wanted to; I had been holding back. I didn't feel secure, had no confidence in myself nor totally trusted his ethics. But I did not want to accept those feelings. I thought we humans are erroneous, trapped and the job is to better and free ourselves. Do not judge others! So I tried for four years in vain, simply because I could not be myself. Not because I was forced by anybody to be different, but because I was not aware that my mind doubted myself.

I had been renovating the bathrooms in my little Majorcan flat and hoping he would feel more comfortable there, I added more details than I had budgeted, not realizing that the external comfort was not the point. Now I found myself with a huge bill three times higher than my original budget. Husband back in the States and I decided not to follow him and instead separate, about to divorce the second time.
In order to solve the financial situation, I spontaneously decided to rent out the flat to make some money and live in a little rented room in town myself.

1 - How It All Began

As a remedy to prevent a major depression, knowing that I had a tendency to ponder too much and identify with old negative emotions, especially sadness, I had signed up for kung fu classes, three times a week for a two-hour-session each and for tai chi the other two days of the week. This would help me to not get lost in thinking and stay connected to my body. At least that was the idea.

So one day, about half a year after separating I walked around Santa Catalina to go for a coffee and I bumped into my old friend.

Having a coffee together we shared what we had been doing the last few years. He had always been very interested in alternative healing techniques, natural health remedies and healthy lifestyle including yoga practices and more. So was I. However, for me it was important to stay away from extremes. I was a firm believer in moderation and consistency. Also, I did not believe in working hard. I had been working hard and it did not work for me. I had burned myself out, then divorced the first time and at the same time been diagnosed with advanced malignant melanoma skin cancer. As a mother of two small children, dying was absolutely not an alternative. I was so tired of all the struggle at the time that I personally didn't mind to go to the other side, but what about the kids? No way! I knew at the time, I had to change something about myself. Inside. And I did. I changed my mind. Later on I worked hard again, but it did not feel like hard work. It felt like a flow, no doubt at all whether I was doing the right thing or not, whether it would pay off or not. Instead, I was driven by an inner source, some kind of an autopilot, that made me run smoothly and keep running without getting tired. My friend, on the other hand, the one I met for coffee that day, had a tendency to see things in a tight frame. Maybe this is what made me relate to him; I knew that way of thinking. I had witnessed that behavior in childhood and had been tight and hard with myself before.

That very day he spontaneously invited me for his birthday party on a boat. His buddy took care of some other friend's boat in Puerto Andratx and invited him to celebrate his birthday there. I accepted and soon after I found myself sitting on a small boat in the harbor of Andratx with a bunch of people I did not know. That day I wanted to go for a swim in the sea and couldn't make it. Arriving to the boat in the evening, the first thing that happened was his buddy asking me to go for a swim. So I did.

Headless Chicken

Turns out that I had a lot of fun with the stranger. We were dancing on the boat, talking, laughing. A similar state of responding to life. We could look at things from a distance and see the good and the bad and still smile. My friend did not quite enjoy seeing us having so much fun. Maybe some kind of jealousy I reckoned. So I just left early that day having enjoyed a couple of really nice hours.

My new boat friend and I stayed in contact and started to meet up here and there. We would watch YouTube videos and talk about what was important to us. At that time it was most important for me to sort myself out. I still thought there was something wrong with me. Convinced something about myself had to be fixed, I started with the most obvious thing that came into my mind: to cure childhood abuse. I ended up researching tantra massage retreats that were supposed to heal sexual issues. Even though I was convinced I would have the guts to do this now, I quickly canceled my first attempt to visit a tantra retreat in India. Talking to the teacher on the phone I had a feeling he was looking for a girlfriend. That was the last thing I needed. Contacting my "still" husband who still could not accept my decision to separate, I shared what was going on with me. I did not want to hold back any longer. Anything. So I also told him about the tantra workshop. He came up with a website of a couple offering healing tantra massage workshops in Eastern Europe that seemed to be more trustworthy. I contacted them, had a Skype conference call and signed up for an eleven-day retreat in Thailand in the following week. I also told my new friend about it.

After eleven days hanging out naked with twenty strangers massaging and being massaged all day long, I came back to Majorca and shared my experiences with my new friend. He had a girlfriend with the same issue to heal, sexual abuse in early age. The most significant experience I made during those eleven days was a memory: I remembered not just the incident of the abuse, but the sensation of how it felt when this man started touching me between the legs. I was six and not allowed to touch myself there. It was such a conflict that my mind had totally pushed away this memory. I remembered the incident the first time when I was thirty-three, twenty-seven years after "forgetting." One day, when my mother was visiting me, I already had children myself, she told me about Mr. K. I will never forget that moment: we were driving up the hill in the outskirts of Munich to the picturesque village we lived at that time. It only took milliseconds to remember

1 - How It All Began

everything after twenty-seven years. She said, "Imagine what happened, how terrible, the daughter of Mr. K. passed away, cirrhosis of the liver, even though she never drank." All of a sudden an incident reappeared in my mind that I did not know had existed. But I could see it clearly in detail. Every word, every action. I remembered a scene that I had experienced as a six-year-old now, at age thirty-three. My father had just passed away a few months earlier. They told me he had a heart attack. My mother was left with three small children, an interior design shop and a mother-in-law she did not get along with. She was on valium, not really present. In that situation she decided to rent out the business to Mr. K. and his family and move to her mother's house. There, the new tenant, Mr. K., renovated my granny's place. That one evening reappeared in my memories: He was there in the living room wearing a white work coat. I was playing under the wallpaper table. I did not know where everybody else was. He said, "I would like to have a girl like you." I said, "But you do have a girl like me." He replied, "But she is not like you, she is more like a boy." Then he touched me between the legs, where nobody was allowed to touch, not even me. And I forgot. I could not cope with the fact that I had allowed somebody to touch me where even I was not supposed to touch myself. Obviously, I did not know that he was going to do so. Nor was I in a position where I could have shouted for help. I was in a position where I feared that I could do something wrong and risk causing more damage. I was in fear that any further disturbances would make the rest of the world that was left collapse. And it was my fault. So I never told anybody and forgot about the incident. But deep down inside, I had a hidden secret that I had forgotten, that made me feel very bad about myself. No matter what I did. Until my mother told me about that man's daughter's death.

That day I remembered, driving with my mom in the car, I thought of myself to be totally nuts. It seemed so crazy to remember such an old story in detail, and yet I knew it was true. A few months later I visited my mom's house, who lived close to Mr. K. I woke up early in the morning and felt so shitty inside that I decided, I cannot live another day unless I fix that issue from the past. I decided to visit that man at lunchtime, knowing that on Saturday he would be done working by noon. I planned to pay him a visit, talk and make peace with the past. Not telling anybody where I was going, not having a clue what I was going to say, I drove twenty kilometers to my former hometown. Parking there, I was trembling so much that I could not get the key

Headless Chicken

into the lock. That was in '98, twenty-seven years after the incident. When I entered Mr. K.'s interior design shop Mrs. K. attended. I told her that I wanted to talk to her husband. So she called him. I told her I wanted to talk with him alone, so she left. He stood there pale and old, not saying a word. So I started: "Twenty-seven years ago," I said, "you came to renovate my grandmother's place. My father had just died. You said to me, you wanted a girl like me. And I said to you that you did have a girl like me. Then you said she wasn't like me. She was more like a boy. Then you touched me. That incident really messed up my life. Now I have come here to give you a chance to forgive." As I talked, he got paler and paler and shook his head. I was amazed how words came out of my mouth without me thinking about what I should say. In the background of my mind thoughts came up like he might deny it all. But it did not matter. All that mattered was that I did my best to fix it. But then I had a feeling that irritated me. I would have loved to just go there and hug him. Having that feeling, my mind judged that was definitively crazy, wanting to hug someone who had abused you. But the moment was so dramatic that nothing really mattered. After finishing those words I could not wait any second longer, so I turned around and headed toward the door. "Manuela," he said. "Wait! … I have also suffered all of my life." That was it.

Then I left, drove to some fields and cried my guts out. The effort did not bring the relief I had hoped for. Maybe it would have been good enough to forgive him quietly. But I did not feel hatred against him. I excused his actions, with my adult's mind, knowing that he was sick, driven, unaware, his own enemy, not wanting to do me harm. I didn't blame him for a life of feeling bad about myself without knowing why, so what should I forgive? I unconsciously blamed myself, not knowing that I could forgive myself as well.

During the tantra workshop in Thailand I remember seeing his hands and feeling the sensation when he touched me down there. I felt the sensation like real. Then my mind kicked in and judged. And I cried for hours. The hard part that made it so tough to accept was that I remembered that feeling, that it felt good to be touched. I had not been hugged that much and especially that area was totally unknown, and unfelt before. It was confusing. As a kid it was absolutely forbidden, yes, yucky, to touch there. That situation had gotten me into a huge conflict and on top of it, it felt good. So bad of a conflict that I could not cope with it and my mind decided to forget.

1 - How It All Began

Shortly after coming back from Thailand, I watched a YouTube video with my friend about Ayahuasca. He seemed to see himself as a do-gooder by sharing what he considered important information with others. I was not into drugs and never considered taking hallucinogens. I once had some kind of out-of-body experience smoking pot where I saw myself passing through a tunnel and seeing my life going backward in a second after losing vision, hearing, senses and finally breath. That gave me a glimpse into what I perceived as "the other side." I never want to miss that experience, since it was most pleasant, to be pure consciousness, observing without any attachment or judgment. Like a good movie. And I no longer doubted about what would happen after death.

I still watched that video about Ayahuasca without any expectation or particular interest. A guy called Scott Peterson talking about the healing properties of Ayahuasca. Nothing of my particular interest really. But something in that video attracted me, so I was tempted to find out more. It was the nature. The green. It could have been anywhere. Googling who put up this video on the web, I found a shamanic healing retreat in the outskirts of Iquitos, Peru. For some unknown reason, I thought I had to go there.

A conversation with my neighbor girlfriend when my father was still around came into my memory: She said when she was grown up she would go to Australia. I said I was going to South America. I did remember this conversation a few times during my life and I had traveled Europe, North America, some parts of Asia and Africa, but never South America. I had not been particularly attracted to South America, did not know where to go, why, and what to look for. But watching that video, I knew I had to go there. I would find out on the way.

That's when the story started. I looked up that website, found the retreat center and also learned that the owner had passed away just a few months earlier. An Australian couple managed the place now. They were looking for a volunteer to translate for the shamans and teach them Spanish. I knew right away: that was me. I sent an email offering my services for work exchange and a few weeks later I sat on the plane, destination for Peru.

2 - The Journey Has Already Started

Knowing That, but not What and Why

The first stop of my travel was Madrid. There, I almost didn't make it to the next leg. Turns out that I needed a visa for a stopover in Miami. How ridiculous, I thought. For stopping on US ground without even being able to leave the airport they make a big deal. At 7 o'clock in the morning at Madrid airport and only having forty minutes layover I couldn't even think clearly what to do next. I had been waiting at the counter to check in my luggage for ten minutes already when I found out that they would not take me on board unless I had a visa. Trying to get a visa online with my newly purchased iPad that I got specifically for Peru did not work out, since I had not yet set up preferences, etc. And doing it on an Iphone 4 was painful, yet seemingly my only solution until I found out a travel agency opening at 7 o'clock in the morning at the Madrid airport. I figured they would work faster to do the online visa application, on their computer than me on my small iPhone screen and I was certainly happy to spend twenty bucks extra for them to do it considering that would be what saves my trip to Peru. So after an exciting half an hour I made it. I got a visa number, had enough time to get my boarding pass and just enough time to make it to the plane. I only had a backpack to take on board and no extra luggage to check. That was the turning point to making it to Miami.

During the overseas leg I wrote in my diary. This came out like hypnotic writing, without thinking:

> 12 —26 — 14
> Madrid Miami.
>
> This journey is all about insights.
> Release resistance and flow.
> Ask questions and get answers.

2 - The Journey Has Already Started

Envision and receive.
Be part of the big picture.
Be and share yourself.

Insights for a mind that tries to understand the laws of the soul in the body.

Ways to expand the local mind and access the big mind, the one mind.

Ways to transcend the limitations of the local mind, filter out the spam on the inbox, to remember true knowledge. Knowledge of one world, connectedness, oneness, no separation, trust in the true laws, laws beyond personal interpretation, trust in life, and in oneself, energy of joy, expansion, evolution, flow of life, truth behind the stories, knowledge beyond the erroneously apparent story, what we seem to perceive via a filtering system, conditionings, judgments, desires, dislikes, that we allowed to be built into our system during this lifetime without ever questioning …

This journey is the about the truth. It had already started watching that YouTube video on Ayahuasca. In fact, it had already started way before. I now recognize the dots that connected to a full picture. Some energetic shifts are happening. Knowing this consciously is exactly what is needed right now. Knowing there is no need to argue, judge, or doubt, but totally trust. During the last two months healing had already happened. But now, it is obvious that there is no going back. Healing will continue. The one that left Majorca will not come back. I will not be the same. I will be one with all. One will come back …

That was what I found myself writing into my diary during the flight to Miami. Reading it afterwards felt weird, almost scary. Something inside of me wrote it without my conscious thinking mind judging. It just came out like that:

This is about the path, living the moment, being present, letting go of concepts, fears and dreams, appreciating what is here and now. Stop fighting life!

Headless Chicken

It had been absolutely amazing for me to witness that some part of me knew a lot without knowing consciously, without thinking, without anybody telling me, nor me reading it somewhere. I had been writing all this down without thinking. And there was some deep insights in those words, insights I had not studied.

It was true: I had been fighting life since I was little. As if I unconsciously tried not only to be different from the picture I had of myself, but to not be at all, be invisible, untouchable and preferably, just not be there at all, if possible. Going to where my father had gone to. I was not conscious of that silent wish at the time. It was more an inner urge or search.

But today, I was very much there, with all senses open, and very present. I continued writing in the diary:

> Start living and enjoying what is now, no matter what. No matter the outer circumstances. This is just like a movie, the real truth is spiritual, the material world is like a projection of the mind. Like a projection on a screen. The reason to be in the body at all is to use that magical God-given power of creativity, use it, play with it, enjoy, create. No body, no play, no manifestation. Do not take the play you create too seriously. Nor your bodily existence. Make it exciting, colorful. Done with pondering, doubting, judging, just let go of programs, clichés, unconscious habits. Bring light in the room. See clearly now! Choose freely in every moment! Open your eyes as if you had never seen before. Be amazed. Accept the miracle. Allow it to happen. This is happening to you, to be free, liberate yourself. You then can help others to allow to free themselves by being yourself. Playfully. All created by the essence. You are always at the right time at the right place, meeting the right people, doing the right thing. Doing nothing can be the right thing too. Just be present.

When I first wrote those notes in my diary during the flight from Madrid to Miami, I do not remember how I felt. I just remember that I did not think when I was writing. It was like hypnotic writing. It just came right out through me. Reading it two years later, it seemed like an entity had been talking through me. Yet, I did not believe it was an external entity, anybody else I had been channeling. First of all,

2 - The Journey Has Already Started

because I don't know how to channel. And secondly, because it felt like I had just tuned in to some information that is available for everybody. It is nothing that I had read in a book. Nothing anybody had told me to do or taught me. I knew I could not know that, at least not from this lifetime. At least not that I could remember learning. I just knew. I knew as if I could remember the truth beyond the conditioned mind. I knew this as if I had already taken Ayahuasca and being able to transcend ego. It felt weird that all these insights came to the surface before I even arrived in the jungle. At that point, I still thought I would go to the Peruvian shamans to interpret and teach Spanish. I had not even thought about participating in Ayahuasca trips. Why should I?

3 - Arriving in Iquitos

About Trust

The next leg was Miami to Lima. I could relax really well during the flight and even sleep a bit. My mind was calm. Ever since I started practicing yoga regularly, I had no problems to spend twenty-plus hours traveling. It is both the mindset, the mental state, and letting go of expectations how things should be, an ability to shut off and just be. And it is a healthy physical condition that makes it easy to travel without pains and complaints.

I arrived late at night in Lima. I took the taxi to a simple hotel near the airport that I had made a reservation for. During overseas travels with jet lag I usually tricked my mind: when I entered the plane or even a few hours earlier I would already think, I am in the time zone I will be traveling to. So even though I relaxed in the plane, I did not sleep but meditated and observed. Sitting in a plane for many hours is a great place for someone like me to have the tranquility to meditate. So I appreciated the time in the plane for being able to meditate with ease.

The next morning my plane left around 10 from Lima to Iquitos. I sat next to a lady from Iquitos who was married to someone from the northern coastline of Peru and was running a surfer hotel there. Interesting, I thought to myself. Maybe I will visit that place sometime while being in Peru. Surfing was on my list of things to do in this lifetime. In fact, surfing had been the only wish I could think of when I got the "certificate" to possibly die within the next few weeks. It was right after divorcing. I went to a dermatologist to take off a wart. She "accidentally" asked me if anyone ever screened my skin. A few weeks later, when I waited for the results of the biopsy in the hospital, I wondered what I would still want to do if I had cancer, while I was still alive. At that point, I totally neglected the possibility that I might have cancer and I figured, if I had that kind of cancer

3 - Arriving in Iquitos

and it had spread, metastasized, there would be no time to fulfill the big wishes and dreams any more. The only thing I could think of was going surfing. Next thing I knew was a doctor telling me "next week might be too late." I realized that nothing really mattered, other than right here, right now. My children were little at the time and the only problem I had was leaving two children without a mother. I was not scared to die. In fact, deep down, unconsciously, I wanted to follow my father since I was a child. Get over the struggle. This hidden desire had never appeared as a wish to end my life purposely like my father had, yet, I had experienced life as a kind of chewy experience, not much flow. I had managed to do what I thought I had to do, studies, languages, business, family. Until the day when I got the message that my life might be over very soon. I knew I had to change something, something inside: my whole setup, my mindset, my habits, my functioning, my neglecting, resigning, trying too hard. I had to become honest and care about my own needs, wishes, preferences. All that I had considered egoistic stuff that I did not want to have or be. I had to face the truth. Say fearlessly NO when I felt it, no longer ignore those parts of myself. I had to stop trying to make things happen just to try to prevent possible damage. I had been driven by fear. Not doing the right thing and possibly becoming guilty "again." Again, because in my childhood mind, I was convinced that I was partly responsible for my father's death. Ridiculous, yet that was what I had learned at that time: do wrong, get punished. Losing a father was clearly a punishment in the mind of that six-year-old.

I had to start living my life out of love to myself and not the life of the others, not out of fear. At that time my whole life experience seemed like an accumulation of obligations. All I knew seemed to be responsibilities. Not noticing that I had missed to be fully responsible for myself. I had to, I had to, I had to. Knowing, or believing to know, what I had to do, kept me in this mindset of forcing things to happen, thinking that I just had to work hard to do the right thing. And my biggest fear was not to do the right thing and become guilty and the world might collapse a little more due to my ignorance or noncompliance with what was the right thing to do. Obviously, that fear was an emotion from past experiences, childish interpretation of a reality that was a lie to start out with. I thought God had taken my father, that must have something to do with me, my wrongdoing. Otherwise he would have taken another father. What I did not know until my early twenties was that he had committed suicide. They told

Headless Chicken

me a lie. They said he had a heart attack. The idea was to protect me. I created my own reality based on a lie, feeling that something was wrong, assuming it was me.

So sitting in the plane next to this lady I remembered my big wish to learn surfing. I knew it was not that important, just another experience and it was okay to do something just for the sake of enjoying it, out of fun. Before, I had constantly questioned what to do and why. I still believe it is good to ask those questions, and yet it is also good to do something for the sake of just enjoying the experience ... But then, once I had my 90% death certificate in my hands, surfing was not important anymore. Very insignificant, in fact.

Iquitos is a city in the middle of the Peruvian Amazon not too far from the border to Brazil and Columbia. You can get there by plane or by boat only. No streets lead there. There is only jungle. And the Amazon River was the only way to get through the rain forest. It sure looks genuine from above, untouched and wild.

As I left the airport, the air seems to get stuck in my throat. It is hot and humid. Outside dozens of moto-taxi drivers are waiting for the voyagers to exit the airport, fighting for a tourist to choose their services. I was supposed to be picked up by the Australians. But nobody was there. Only lots of loud taxi drivers who want to give me a ride into town. Speaking Spanish helps to make it clear that I am waiting for somebody to pick me up. The noise volume is intense. Only once I dare to think: what if they don't come ... ? It felt like nothing really matters. I will know what to do when the time is right. So I just waited. Fifteen or twenty minutes later a moto-taxi arrived with two girls in it. I knew it was them. They picked me up and together we drove into the center of Iquitos where we waited for some other people to arrive. The hostel they had picked as a meeting place. There I met a guy who had been at the retreat center for a couple of weeks and then left, to celebrate Christmas in Iquitos. Later I found out that he had been a multiple addict to anything one can think of: sex, drugs, and alcohol. He came to heal from addictive behavior with the help of the spiritual master plant Ayahuasca. Waiting for a couple of hours at the hostel I got to know a few more people who had arrived and waited for a ride to the retreat center in the middle of the jungle, away from everything. One guy from London, in fact, he was German, like me. A film producer, son of a Peruvian father and a German mother.

3 - Arriving in Iquitos

Interesting combination! We connected instantly without talking much. I was told that there would be no dinner at the retreat, so I better get some food now. During the days they did Ayahuasca ceremonies, there was no dinner. For a reason. Vomiting during ceremony was even worse if you ate dinner, the whole trip was harder to get on. They organized two days in a row celebrating Ayahuasca ceremonies, then a day off. The days on, there was no dinner. That night there would be a ceremony, so no dinner at the retreat center. So I went with my new Peruvian-German friend and got some local food from next door. Very different everything.

Once the other two people whom we had been waiting for had arrived, we went in several moto-cars to what they called the harbor, a strip down by the river. Approximately a hundred fragile, old wooden stairs led down to the riverbank to get to the boats. The people of the retreat center I went with had come with their own boat from the retreat center. It took one and a half hours from the center in the jungle into Iquitos to pick up clients and one and a half hours back. A simple handmade canoe-type wooden boat with a simple, loud motor and a palm roof to protect from sun and rain. Fully packed with passengers and luggage we headed into the jungle. Everything seemed slower. The Amazon is amazing. Big and powerful.

Finally arriving at the retreat center, the staff welcomed me and the other guests and I was led to my house, a beautiful, huge, open wooden hut in the middle of the jungle. No other huts in sight. Everyone lived in an individual huge, round wooden two-story hut, with a bathroom. Everyone had their own house to stay in, dozens of meters away from the others, hidden in the jungle.

My house was very close to the ceremony house where Ayahuasca ceremonies were held. You couldn't see it from my place, though. I could feel the atmosphere differently when something was going on over there, when they were in ceremony. Strange, almost miraculous. Nothing I could explain with words. Then there was El Centro building close to the river, where everybody met, ate and had consultations with the shamans. There was the open kitchen, dining room on the first floor, library, and space to hang out in hammocks or chairs and sofas. There were approximately ten full-time workers employed who took care of food, supplies, laundry, cleaning and renovating broken parts of the wooden buildings such as leaking palm tree roofs, broken-

Headless Chicken

down floors, etc. There were two cooks and a "washer," a lady who did nothing but wash every day and every hour of the day, for every host of the retreat and the managers. She was my age. She was humble. She looked worn out.

I loved my cottage, a totally round, hand-built, wooden construction with mosquito fences all around. Nothing was straight. Everything was handmade, slanting, imperfect, not machine-made. The hut, the bed, the little table, the chairs, the bathroom shower, the hammock.

4 - First Ayahuasca Experience

Just Do It

Once I arrived and met the shamans I immediately felt like home. I was not only intrigued, but there was no more question about whether I would participate during ceremonies or not. Before I did not even consider taking Ayahuasca. I thought this trip was about being in nature, learning from people. To take the medicine or not I had not contemplated. I had just gone with my gut feeling, confident that once I get to the next crossing, or decision to make, I would feel what is right for me. I had no intention to trip in order to see beautiful pictures like an LSD trip. What for? A quick buzz? I had no idea that there was still something to heal, thinking I had already done everything I could when it comes to healing. Not knowing that there was more work necessary to heal the soul and it might be nothing I could solve by doing, but by letting go, which is so much more difficult, because you can't let go forcefully. In other words: not knowing that allowing is the work. And also not knowing how to allow. How could I get my ego to allow me to pass through? Especially after suppressing all that "nasty stuff" a life long ...

So here I am, ready to participate in an Ayahuasca ceremony out of the blue as if this was the most common thing in the world. I had eaten no sugar or salt, nor meat nor had I drunk alcohol. That is the Ayahuasca diet one should follow. Wrapped into a long-sleeve shirt and long pants, to protect against mosquitos, wearing rubber boots to walk through the muddy grounds over to the ceremony hall. I took a bottle of water, mosquito spray, toilet paper, and a torch, since there was no light anywhere. In the rain forest the moon does not shine through in most places. At 7:30 p.m., already pitch black, a guide comes to pick me up and bring me over to the ceremony hall. Arriving there in this huge round, open hand-made wood building, they had prepared mattresses on the floor for every person joining the ceremony set up in a half circle around the shamans with a bucket next to it. Vomiting was part of the deal. In the middle of the circle a candle is lit until the ceremony starts. The shamans wear traditional clothing. One man is a third-generation Shipibo native shaman from Pucallpa named Francisco. The other shaman, Don José, was a local from the next village down the river. They smoke local tobacco, a ritual to protect from bad spirits. I can hardly stand the smoke, even though the huge construction has no walls, it is more of an open space with a roof.

Once everybody has arrived, the shamans explain to the new guests what would be happening. Basically, to trust in the process of how the plant medicine works. So that is what I do. I have no fear at all about this experience.

A few years earlier, I had experienced the near-death experience smoking some potent pot in high altitude. As I mentioned before, I didn't do pot or any other drugs. That day in the mountains, I just did it and lost consciousness to the extent of seeing my life going backward and getting a glimpse to how it is when there is only one's consciousness without any attachment to a body. Ugly to get there at first, losing control over the body, but unforgettable and soothing thereafter. Safe. Peaceful.

Ayahuasca is potent, different from pot. Something tells me I have nothing to fear and it is absolutely okay for me to just do it. So I do it super confident without any expectation, fear or goal.

They give me a beginner's dose, which is a quarter of a shot. The taste is awful. Then I lie down on my mattress, cover myself with a blanket and close my eyes. After some time taking Ayahuasca medicine, the shamans walk around and blow Agua de Flores or something similar that smells like perfume and alcohol toward each of us. They come around with that bottle, take some of that stuff in their mouth and blow it over everybody, especially onto the head area. Some of it they give us into the hands to rub it into the palms. That liquid smelled like spirits. And it seemed to kick-start something else through the olfactory organ. It is supposed to protect as well. As they put some of it toward my face and throat, it feels like a message for the senses, a trigger. The candle is off by now. Then, they start singing and the magic starts. I don't remember how long it took that very first time, but since I had no expectation or comparison, the whole process starts

4 - First Ayahuasca Experience

without me doubting it might not work for me. I see sprinkles of colored lights, like beautiful fireworks turning into colorful spirals moving in three or more dimensions, twisting, swirling, playfully turning. Shape-changing sparks from square to triangle to stars and to forms I had never seen before nor could I describe them. "Medicina poderosa," they sing, powerful medicine. I feel a bit sick, but don't vomit.

I open my eyes eventually, all gone, close my eyes again, all coming back immediately. Swirling spirals like spirograph designs filled with magical colors in each hole. I can look into it and it goes deeper. I don't know if it goes deeper into nowhere, or if it is coming toward me, the observer. It appears to me as if observing the process had an impact on the observed, like an interactive perspective: That what I see and I were playing together, a game I was included in somehow without directly interfering physically, just my consciousness. I can shift from going inward, or going outward, away, into the depths, back to going toward me. I can also change perspective in a different way and look from the side. And suddenly, I see ugly muddy colors, snakes and bugs, made of spiral textures. I notice they are just as good, as long as I did not label them. "Go play with them. None is better or worse." Very weird, but at the moment, I did not judge a thing.

Then, I see my father's face, his eyes. He is around all the time. Humble eyes. Full of love. I look for my mother, but she is not there. She is just not there, not available to be seen, like disconnected from the game of something. Still no need to interpret or judge, I just don't. Find myself rubbing my solar plexus heavily, then heart chakra. Very strongly. An urge to heat up that spot. I am all involved in seeing far into the universe and suddenly rub my physical body that is lying there in the ceremony hall. It feels like a release of energy there, which has been locked up for a long time. Snuggling like a baby, hugging myself, loving myself, free, independent, complete. Feel like the world was my womb. Feel safe and sound. No limitations other than the ones I decide to create in my own mind. It is me creating and changing this picture I see.

I have no idea how much time has passed. The light in the middle being is lit once the shamans stop singing. That is the sign that the ceremony has ended. Slowly, slowly one guest after the other leaves the room in the next hour or two. I just want to go home to my hut,

Headless Chicken

go to bed and sleep. I feel very sick and my body is struggling to work like normal. Desperately I try to get on my feet. But the body just does not cooperate. Everything is still kind of swirling and I am very uncomfortable in my body, just want to go home, finish the process, now, and sleep. But I can't. Every time I try to get on my feet, my knees are shaking so badly that I lose balance and have to lie down again. Holding the feet with the hands lifting the bottom up first, I try to get more stable, but as soon as I lift the upper body, the knees start shaking that hard that I can't keep balance. So I give in, lie down, and decide to wait until the body is ready to move. My mind does not want to surrender, I desperately want to go home, sleep, digest, and be finished for the day, but I just have no choice other than wait until I can walk again. Interestingly enough, I have full faith that this would happen sooner or later. All it would take is the needed time.

Everybody has gone, except one of the shamans and one of the guides, when I finally get on my feet. It was probably after 2 by then. I am so glad that the guide is there to take me home. He offers his arm but I don't want to accept. Until I start to try walking down the endless-seeming wooden staircase from the first floor to the ground floor. Holding myself with two hands on the railing, I still don't have enough strength and stability to make it safely down to the ground, so I finally accept his help. It seems to take forever to get to my hut which is only sixty or eighty meters away. We cross a wooden bridge and go up the small hill to reach the eight-edges house. It is incredibly hard to cross that bridge and make my way up the hill. I tell my guide to leave now, I will find my way home. So he stays back with the torch and I keep going by myself. When I reach the house and know it is definitely my place, I keep going around, corner by corner. The entrance is in the back of the house. Every house is roundish, with eight edges or so like a STOP sign. Counting corners, I keep going and going but never reach the door. That's when I freak out a bit. An imagination of snakes comes into my mind and I worry having to sleep in the jungle on the ground with the snakes.

That moment I instantly remember that situation when I was a child. I slept in my sister's room. She was a baby in her crib and I slept on the sofa bed in her room. As a kid, I sometimes woke up in the night while I was already on my feet, thinking it was time to get up and prepare for the day. That night I was sleeping in my baby sister's room. I knew it was not time to get up and I remembered being in her room and

4 - First Ayahuasca Experience

not in mine. Since I could not find the light switch and didn't want to wake up the baby anyway, I decided to search for the bed in the dark. It couldn't be too hard. Once I found the curtains, there was the window and right next to it, should be the bed, I thought. But once I found the window next to it, there should have been the bed. It was upright! That freaked me out. The bed could not possibly be upright. It took quite a while that night until I had figured it out: there was another glass door with curtains in that room, and what I thought to be the bed was the cupboard. After that, it was easy to find the bed. Why did I remember this? Because it was a typical example of how one can be misled by believing what you think is true, how one can freak out and lose confidence.

But now at night in the Peruvian jungle, it is not just about freaking out. There is a very real possible problem and danger: It is not safe to sleep on the ground in the jungle! All I know is that I can't find the entrance to the house. It feels as if I had gone around the whole house once at least without finding the freaking door. So I call the guide to come back and thank God, he is still around and helps me out. He opens the door for me and leaves. Finding the light switch with the torch is easy, but the light at that time of night is not working. The generator was only operating a few hours longer, after the ceremony. So I find my way with the torch. All is new there. Also being on Ayahuasca ... moving from one spot to another is not easy. I still have to use the restroom, another challenge on wobbly legs. Then I manage to get up the uneven wooden staircase without railings, undress and find my bed. I get upstairs on all fours. Once I make it to the bed I feel relaxed. But the journey keeps going on in my mind all night. I am still tripping. No way to stop. Keep traveling. I still don't have my regular perception back and my mind is unsettled and wild, looking for the comfort of the habitual "box." I hear noises of the jungle and I perceive them much louder than ever. Huge leaves falling from the trees sound like men walking around the house. Animals making noises I've never heard before. I notice potential fear and decide to let go of that emotion, knowing that I don't know anything, pictures coming up, ideas, possibilities, assumptions. Amazing, how it is possible to just detect the illusion of fear and let go! Still, those sounds and pictures in my mind kept going all night long. And I just observe without attachment, and without judgment, everything other than comfortable, it just is as it is.

Headless Chicken

The next day I felt drained and exhausted. At 7 o'clock in the morning the kitchen helper came to bring me a small plate of fresh fruit to the door. I was happy to see him. And I could eat the food, I did not feel sick anymore. I was hungry. I must have burnt loads of calories, plus I had no dinner. It was perfect. Just perfect. Even though I couldn't get back to my regular state of mind during the entire day, whatever that was. And maybe that was exactly the way it was supposed to be, by nature. I later reckoned that this was exactly what it takes to let go of programs, concepts, and previously thought ideas, somehow wearing out the old form to become empty and allow new, empty space to see the bigger picture.

During the day, without thinking about it, the meaning of what I had experienced came into my mind. It just dropped down into my conscious mind. I realized that all I had seen, the beautiful stuff and the ugly stuff, was made out of the same material, the same moving energy. It was up to me how I would look at things. This is the nature of duality, the three-dimensional world of the two sides to everything, odd and even, good and bad, black and white. Everything has two sides to it and it is up to me how I look at it, how I respond to it and most of all: what I choose. This is the law of the material world. It is all made of the same stuff, showing up as different shapes. And I am in a position to reshape it, the way I "look" at things, how I choose to interact with this energy mass.

I wondered what else there was to be discovered after this profound insight.

By 10 o'clock everybody would meet up at the center for breakfast and hang out for a couple of hours. People got to know each other, shared their stories and their experiences.

It was interesting to observe, how we compared one story with somebody else's story, especially when it came to people sharing their Ayahuasca experience. Soon I decided to stop sharing my experiences in detail, since I felt that limited the possibilities for newcomers to experience their own individual insights that they were ready for at the time. They might get stuck in expectations, missing their own meaning of their whole trip.

4 - First Ayahuasca Experience

It is quite interesting to observe that this plant medicine seems to give a person exactly whatever that person is ready for at that specific time. No standard program, like a regular pill, more like an intelligence working behind. But is it the biochemical substance of the plants in combination with the sound waves that create this "intelligent" process or are these substances just opening us up to something else that then can work perfectly through us? And is this process safe?

Some people came in for a few days and others for a few weeks and everybody—well, almost everybody—seemed to receive their messages, insights and healing just in time before leaving. Some had bad experiences, no healing, nothing "satisfying" them. It seemed like nature gives you exactly what you need and what you can cope with. There is no set time. The time is always perfect. And for some, that moment just has not yet come. Like that one girl who was suffering from depression since childhood. She was convinced nothing had changed for her with the plant medicine.

People around her perceived her differently, but she could not feel it, as if she was addicted to believing her depression is what she is. Saying that, it makes a lot of sense to me: Is not depression a suppressing of what we call negative emotions over a long period of time and the body creating biochemical consequences accordingly? Like a mental and emotional habit, the mind trying to take control by suppressing emotions as a consequence of unbearable feelings once upon a time. And maybe this leads to the extent of habitually trying not to feel what really is, afraid of "negative" feelings or emotional memories, but thinking or interpreting the issue away. But thinking only one can eventually get stuck in that pattern of thinking, pondering, judging, evaluating, searching, and suffering. That comes not without chemical consequences in the body, hormones responding to the cycle of no outlet from constant thinking and constant stress. Then, we end up in a serious mess inside, which not only feels but is very real on a physical level. We know what we know and we are bound to that knowing to a level that we don't allow a new belief in our system: hope, faith and the possibility to change. That is what keeps us trapped. That what we think we know. That is what keeps us away from God's grace, from love and from healing. No belief, no hope, no healing. If we don't manage to have faith and believe, nothing can help us, not even Ayahuasca. As soon as the old program of thinking and beliefs kicks in, that "knows," all hope and all potential is gone. Trapped. That's how I see it today.

Headless Chicken

That girl used to get very annoyed when people told her she looked so much better or even dared to give her tips to change something in her everyday life to change how she felt. She thought nobody knew what was going on inside of her and what she had gone through mentally and chemically. She was like married and loyal to the past and to the conditioning. Hopeless, highly studied and very knowledgable. I didn't get involved with her too much and decided to just let her be the way she was at the time without trying to help or change her. Accept, allow her to be. Allow myself to be. Through my filters of perception it seemed as if she felt taken seriously, when nobody messed with her disease, like some kind of silent agreement and maybe even a small amount of confidence.

5 - Second Ayahuasca Experience

Embracing Duality

After that first night I kind of got the idea behind duality. I saw and felt it clearly. Yet, it was still difficult for me to accept the concept of good and bad in the material world, away from Ayahuasca. I had tried all my life to only see the good in people and in myself and ignore or excuse all the bad. It didn't work. That habit had gotten me into abusive and dangerous situations quite a few times. Good and bad is still there. Here it is about our "freedom" to choose, talk the truth, act upon it responsibly. Somehow I had chosen to ignore bad and that is a no-go.

The second night being in the jungle was a night off. That night there was no Ayahuasca ceremony. Two nights on, one night off. That was good, because it took me all day to recover from that first night and get back into my body. I felt so weak that I even couldn't practice any yoga or tai chi. The only activity I did was swimming a little in the river at sunset. The ladies of the house, all of my age, in their forties, at this time in the evening went down to the river to first wash their clothes and then themselves. There was Lucy the chef and Berna the washer. Berna was exactly my age and looked approximately ten years older. She had children who lived ten minutes away by boat, fifteen years younger than mine. She spent most of her time at the refugio working. Washing, washing, washing. By hand. Making a living. Most weekends she went home for one day only. She was a blessing. Always smiling, kind, and helpful. So was Lucy. In fact, we made friends, Lucy and I. Lucy called me "La Barbie." I guess because of my long legs and blonde hair. Very funny. If anybody else had called me "the Barbie," I would have felt offended, my lower mind interpreting that means something similar to "blonde and dumb." From her it was kind of sweet. We met almost every night at sunset, which was early evening. While I swam, they washed. When I came out of the water, we chatted.

Headless Chicken

I really don't remember exactly what we were talking about every evening, but it felt like talking to old friends. It was important to me and it was important to them to share. I felt blessed to know these people. They were honest and very direct, yet without blaming others, putting them down or making them feel bad. I learned a lot from these two ladies. Especially from Lucy.

During the day, I had heard someone scream badly. So badly that I even considered searching for the manager's home to inform them about someone being in total distress. I just had no energy. Later I found out that they knew about the guy screaming and had decided to not interfere. It was Jason, the kid I met in Iquitos at arrival. He had been at the refuge for ten days or so and then went into town to celebrate Christmas. There, he had gone back to alcohol and drugs for only a few days. When he came back to do Ayahuasca healing his issues got really bad, worse than before. He really suffered. He screamed in a way that I could hear it approximately one kilometer away in the jungle. It gave me goosebumps. What the heck must have happened, for someone to be screaming like that? It sounded like he was paying hard for his return to drugs. It sounded like he had become very aware of what was right for him and he agreed to accept the information. Screaming gave him a way to relieve the pain of having hurt himself. After listening to him for some time, I realized that it was releasing for him, to allow himself to feel it, accept, and let it go. He was a nice kid in his early twenties. Chunky, intelligent and sweet. Unfortunately, intelligence doesn't seem to really help to master one's lower self. We had some good conversations. We inspired each other. I didn't feel less of an addict than him when it comes to compulsive thinking habits. So I did feel, we are made out of the same stuff. Call it one mess or one mass or one blessing.

The next morning we still got fruit at 7 o'clock even though we did have dinner and no ceremony. It was delicious. Very little and very delicious. Having less variety of food, less sweets or unhealthy fats, it felt luxurious to get served this small plate of freshly cut fruit in the middle of the jungle. I enjoyed every single bite. Mango, papaya, melon and grapes. I used to sit downstairs on the ground floor of my house to have breakfast. Then went back up the hand-carved, wooden half-circle stairs to the first floor to either relax a little longer in bed, or draw, or write. Call it inner work. On the day with more physical energy I would move my body smoothly, do a bit of yoga or tai chi.

5 - Second Ayahuasca Experience

During the day, I hung out some time at the center and met with other guests, interpreted for clients who wanted to communicate with the shamans or taught Spanish to the couple who ran the place since only a few months. This Ayahuasca tripping or ceremony work was very intense for everybody. And almost everybody had questions. I had the honor to translate very personal stuff between visitors and shamans. A couple of years before, I had visited a workshop in Germany to become an accredited alternative healer in that country. My intention was to find out what was the difference between someone who is considered or diagnosed to be sick and someone who is just out of balance. I never attempted to become an accredited healer in the state of Germany because I did not want to participate in what I saw as a sick system to start out with. As if it was about administering diseases, whereas my intention was to focus on allowing the perfect essence, the one everybody comes with, back to the surface and teaching healthy habits. I still wonder why they call it health insurance and not sickness insurance. BTW, in Germany they call it richness insurance. Failing the exam by one point tells it all ... What I learned was that there was not such a thing as a clear line between whole or healthy and sick. Depending on the International Classification of Diseases in use, the ICD, certain symptoms that used to be "tolerated" as "normal" may be recognized as diseases at some point, or vice versa. I always wondered what criteria makes them change their minds. I truly wished it wasn't the pharmaceutical industry ... A practical definition and criteria for being healthy is to be functional in life and that sure sounds like a machine more than a human.

Depending on where you live, e.g. in Europe or in the States, they use different classification systems. Whereas some experience or behavior is considered to be sick over here, in another country it can be healthy. My experience was that people I had worked with as a "walking coach" (a vocation I chose and developed after surviving cancer) were just as healthy or sick as some people that came to me as part of their intense therapies with psychologists. The people who did not go to therapy and were not diagnosed to be "sick" seemed to be more in charge of themselves. They took responsibility that they were out of balance and they were willing to change something about themselves. So they hired me as their life coach to help them change themselves. They did not expect a doctor or therapist to do the job for them. Obviously, that attitude helps to get back into balance and into your own power.

The "health system" seems to be keeping patients irresponsible. Operate the hip, come back with the other hip soon. Take the pill and keep taking it. Nobody seems to give a shit about helping these people to change something. OK, the job has to be done and this is exaggerated, but it is alarming. And there are some great doctors and alternative therapists out there who really care more about people than about their status and feel it is their job to help patients become responsible and in charge of their lives.

When experiencing cancer in 2000, I was devastated, knowing that I had to change something essential. I just didn't know what and how. For the first time in my life, at age thirty-five, I went to the German unemployment office to tell them I needed some kind of postgraduate education. Even though I had an MBA degree, spoke four languages fluently, and had ten years of business experience as a managing director of a publishing company, inside of me was such a mess that I felt it didn't make any sense to send me to any job interview in that state. I felt useless at that point. And I needed to find meaning in what I would do. I needed some kind of reprogramming. A total reboot. Something that made my mind think differently. That I saw very clearly. That's what I told them at the unemployment office. The lady behind the desk told me that it was a very bad time to ask for postgraduate education since the budget had been spent. Plus, for people with my qualifications, there was no budget anyway. However, she said, she wondered if anything is available last minute … She went around the corner and picked up a sheet. It had turned out that just a day earlier one participant had canceled a real cool seminar called "Mental Power" and one spot had opened up. I would participate in that one month, eight hours a day coaching training! The training happened to take place just behind where I lived with my children at the time, therefore it was easy and convenient for me to participate. Also, it started the very following week. Great! My lovely Greek neighbors agreed to take the children home from kindergarten and school and watch them for a couple of hours after school, until I would finish at 5. The following week I started my new training. Some magic seemed to happen once I opened up that door, meaning, once I had become responsible for myself, gained hope, faith and was open for change: During the course I had to give a talk. I had never ever given a talk, not at school nor at University. I felt very, very uncomfortable to give a talk. Ashamed, timid, not good enough. Too many people talking too much was the argument my mind made up to justify the old emotion and the habit

5 - Second Ayahuasca Experience

of not daring to break through. On the other hand, I was absolutely sure that it was really important for me to open my mouth now. Now or never. This is the only chance. The last chance. If I wouldn't dare now, I would keep on shutting up, staying trapped for the rest of my life. That's how I felt. I needed to talk my truth and share something that was important for me to share.

I had ten minutes preparation time and ten minutes talking time. All it took was something that I believed in and that I felt was really important for the others to know about. Something really helpful, worthwhile to share. So I talked about my personal remedy to walk in the woods for hours and hours, during my worst times. I walked until my monkey mind had given up and I had found inner peace and tranquility. I wrapped the story into a business environment and called the talk "walking during lunch break." Pros, cons, conclusion. Easy. Once I started, still feeling shitty, I saw the shine in the audience's eyes. It didn't take a minute to stop feeling stupid, because I was connected with my listeners on a subtle level. Maybe with their hearts. Something connected. And it was not the arguments, it was not due to the pros and cons why they gave me their total attention. They were interested, they felt something and I could feel it. Plus, I really believed this might be very important information for some of them. After that talk five people approached me and asked me if we could do a walk during lunch break thereafter until the end of the month. So we did. That was the beginning of the walking coach business, my mission and passion. At the same time a friend of mine, a personal trainer, asked me to work with one of her clients. She said she really couldn't deal with this lady, she drove her nuts, she was so difficult. She figured I was more diplomatic and in control of myself, I would be able to deal with her. I wasn't interested in offering personal training at all. Work for weight loss and vanity. However, I decided to have an open mind and give it a shot. There must be something else behind a weight problem than just calories and it was my job to help change. So I agreed. Soon after, I had my first client as a walking coach. After finishing the seminar, I wrote a business plan for my newly invented business. The city of Munich liked the idea and sponsored 50% of the Social Security costs during the first six months. If they believe in me, I thought, I can do it. I spent every free hour of the day during the week to develop a website and flyers. It wasn't so much about marketing, it was more about convincing myself of the importance of that work I planned to offer. I wanted to help people connect with themselves, getting out of the head, into the body, into the feelings, into the heart. I had witnessed how one can get lost, reducing oneself to a thinking functional machine-type thing. It has cost me burnout, marriage, and cancer. It was important for me to do this work, to share what I had learned. Soon after starting, I had reached my objectives that I had forecasted within six months. And I was making enough money to pay the bills within half a day of work and could spend the rest of the day taking care of the children and household. During this time I realized that I can do what I want to do. The only question is: what do you really want? I had the desire to leave the city and raise my children at a sunny, safe place, preferably near the seaside. Italy or Spain would be cool. In 2003 we moved from Germany to Majorca within three months after having the intention. In the meantime, during many years as a walking coach, I accompanied hundreds of people from many countries in very different settings.

Now, in the jungle, it felt like it was meant for me to interpret for those people looking for healing from the plants and the shamans. I had experience, compassion, and patience and I spoke languages. Many of these searchers were truly grateful that I was there. There were people from all over the world, of different ages, different social classes and professions. I felt we were all the same. Looking for the very same thing. Love, peace, joy. Overcome the habit of suffering from judging situations as not good or bad.

During those months we shared so many hours, so many different people, stories, and difficulties to overcome, that I felt blessed to have been chosen to accompany all these beautiful people.

At the beginning I felt bad about myself for feeling annoyed about some people's behavior. I had judged myself for judging others. My inner critic was working hard to criticize myself for criticizing others. How crazy is that monkey mind? If there is no real problem, it can produce one.

That night we have no dinner and were picked up at 7:30 for the Ayahuasca ceremony. I am confident and relaxed. This night I take a little bit more of the plant medicine. Same procedure as the first time: once everybody is at their spot, and the shamans do their initiation rituals, then the candlelight is gone and they start singing the icaros, the traditional songs. Don José sings in Spanish language, Francisco

5 - Second Ayahuasca Experience

in Shipibo, a bizarre-sounding native language. Even though I don't understand a word of Shipibo, it was as if the message came to me anyway, about pain, or injustice or joy. The heart can understand.

It is easy that second time to get into a trance, let go of thinking and just observe what is, beyond the thinking mind. This time, shapes are tiny, subtle, sweet, sensitive, sacred. I can choose to focus or not focus, look at it or look out, or away. It is my choice what I focus on. And this is the whole message: it is my choice. What I focus on is what I see; it is absolutely okay, whatever I choose, it is my freedom to choose. I have the power with my focus, vision, concentration and breath to switch on or off. Breathing makes the energy move, like blowing air in the fire. Exhaling, it starts moving stronger. The pictures I see start moving according to the way I breathe. I experiment with inhaling and exhaling.

It is fun to observe, how I can direct those pictures with my own breath. I play. Not searching for anything, just playing. I feel okay, I'm not sick. Again, I have no idea or control over time. I am just observing. There is no me. Me is some kind of observing eye and yet not separate from the process. After the ceremony ends I still stay longer. Because again, I can't really get up. I try to get up and all of a sudden, it seems like an old pile of heavy stones shooting from the center of my guts through my throat to my mouth. An explosion of a plug. Unplugging forcefully, as purging. Like a very old blockage. I vomit what feels like a handful of stones that were stuck in my guts since many, many years. It's okay. It's a relief.

I feel free and powerful. Try to go home right after ceremony and again, need several trials to finally balance my body on my feet. Again, can hardly make it down the stairs. Accept and go with what is, with less resistance. Again, I need the help of the guide to assist me down the stairs, bring me home and show me the door to my house. This night, I gladly accept his offer to help at the first time.

Even though I feel very very sick it feels kind of funny to walk like a drunk. Waggling from one leg to another and having such a difficult time to do the bathroom business. Getting this body up the staircase without falling down. Undressing, finding the bed and the opening of the mosquito net.

Headless Chicken

Again, it is a rough night with lots of loud noises from the rain forest and the busy mind not sleeping but continuing to process all night long.

6 - Third Ayahuasca Night

Permission to Do What I Like

During the day, I slowly slowly get used to the idea of possibly going to do the same thing during the next three months without getting anxious. I had mixed feelings: the jungle is amazing. But how would it be to spend three months without Internet, distraction, the amenities of Western life and hardly "doing" anything? Would I fall back into pondering too much, like I did when I was a child? What if I doubted that this was the right decision? Would I be able to cope with upcoming emotions without the possibility to distract or run away? Or what if I even started believing there was no use to all of this, the experience in the jungle, the search, or even life as such? I now had a lot of time without any distraction to figure out what I am about and how life works. Would I get the answers within the time staying?

I had already gotten the answer to duality, what else is there to discover after that? My mind was going fast, occupied with what I thought were the most important questions ever.

On the huge land that belonged to the retreat, there was one wide area that felt different, magical. Whenever I passed through there to get to my house, I felt like in a trance-like state more connected to nature. My thinking mind was shut off and I merely knew it was me, or my body walking through that area. It felt like I am the observer who sees the whole picture, which included me, my body. It felt like the true me is more than the body named Manuela that comes with her feelings and thinking mind. It felt like I am not only the observer, but part of all this, connected and Manuela's thinking mind had a break. Manuela's body was part of that picture. Like an actor on the stage play. It all played together and it didn't really matter too much what the play was about. It was just a play. Nothing to be taken too seriously. Sit down, lay back and enjoy the ride. You are the audience, the actor and the director. If you forget, you end up thinking and feeling as if that stage play was the real deal, but it is just a projection. And you might take it very seriously. And risk to reduce yourself to being the actor who did not choose anything with no power over his energy whatsoever, a victim of circumstances. Where in reality, this is just more of a play, temporary with us creating it in every moment.

As soon as I had passed through this area, it felt like I started forgetting again, back in my lower level of awareness, trapped in the thinking judgmental mind. Especially, when I walked toward the center and met up with other people. Walking in the opposite direction, toward my house, I seemed to be able to stay longer in this state of elevated consciousness. Maybe because there was less distraction. Different energy exposure. More silence and nature.

I spent most of the days very quietly. At the beginning, I would regularly give Spanish lessons to the managers. One of the reasons why I was there was to teach them. I used the technique I had learnt in Majorca: Alpha State Learning. Help the student get into a very relaxed state of mind with the help of relaxation techniques such as yoga, tai chi, Qigong or guided meditation. Similar to what I had learned in hypnosis. Once the student reached a very relaxed state, the mind would open up for learning something new. That opened the door for the learning process to thrive, since the inner critic would not interfere all the time using all the energy for questioning whether they thought they had learned that vocabulary yet or not, whether they knew the grammar behind that sentence or not and whether they would remember that or not. They could just open up and let it flow. It was a much more playful way of learning. Less resistance. However, one of the two students, the lady, was not open to experiment with this new-fashioned, almost revolutionary and uncontrolled way of learning. Not controlling the process seemed to stressed her out. I tried not to assume anything, just accept. Soon after, I found out that they faced an intense personal situation out there in the jungle. Obviously, that made it hard to be able to let go. Let go of the old way of learning and open up to less conventional, "uncontrolled" methods. After they had shared their personal story and situation with me, everybody had less expectations and was okay to take the learning process and progress easy, instead of adding another load on their plate. For her, we switched from the alpha method to conventional books. The best way for them to learn, once they had learned some

6 - Third Ayahuasca Night

basics, was taking them into town and "play." The only rule was: do not speak English! This way the inner critic was tricked out, because they were so busy with focusing on expressing the message they wanted to get over, that it wasn't that important if they used the right grammar. Buy a sandwich. Exchange money. Ask for the way …

Doing Ayahuasca two out of three days was intense and mostly the process of inner work continued during the day energetically, wanting to or not. I was sick and weak in such a way that I was not able to do much else than just be and listen, to others, nature, inside. Just not do anything. Just be. That was probably also a reason why the couple often canceled Spanish classes at short notice. Besides their personal problems, work with Ayahuasca required a lot of energy. So we decided that they would approach me the very day when they had enough extra energy for learning. It was an interesting agreement. Our Western minds are so used to planning and knowing or wanting to know what will be happening next, that it felt uncomfortable at the beginning. It felt like my life was not my own, my time was not my own either, having to be on call all the time. My issue! So I decided to play with that and experiment to overcome that idea of limitation. Letting go of that subtle resistance to not knowing what would happen that day. Not to become more flexible, I was rather too flexible, but to become more free and possibly consider to say no, when it wasn't right for me. I noticed that I had let go expectations as well. I no longer worried whether I could make them speak Spanish after those three months or not. Whereas before, I would have felt bad about myself for not being able to fulfill their expectations in their complicated and difficult situation. Shall I now feel bad about myself, or just learn to grow beyond my former beliefs, irritations and limiting programs? I decided to let go and grow, even though I did not know how and whether I would be able to do so or not. So that for me was the first noticeable impact, the glimpse into the other world during Ayahuasca had on me while experiencing a three-dimensional life in the body, the everyday's experience.

I had brought an iPad with ebooks, drawing apps, music, paint, and a yoga mat. I hardly used anything. These three months were not so much about doing, but about learning, understanding and being.

* * *

Headless Chicken

This is the third ceremony. I choose to take half a cup of "plant medicine" like the night before and not increase the dosage. There is no rush, I may as well have a softer experience instead of kicking ass. No pushing hard in order to perform better and to make the most of the situation. That strategy doesn't always work out. In fact, that's how I burnt out and weakened my own system! Never totally relaxing, always in control, in charge, somehow worrying about what to worry about to make sure to be safe, anxious most of the time. Never totally at ease and relaxed.

So that night only take half a cup like the night before. Don't push it. Allow ...

Even though my mind wondered whether I will be able to enter the trip quickly or whether my ego might block the entrance to the experience, I get there with ease. This time, I see subtle images again. Time seems to pass very fast. I puke. Right at the beginning in the first hours or so. It's okay for this stuff to come out. Even though it's quite disgusting, it also feels cleansing. It's okay. No judgments, no suffering! Easy. The experience is not as thrilling as the first time. What I see is less astonishing, less amazing, compared to the first time. Ha! Comparing sets in. Expecting... Interesting! As if repetition defeats effect. That's how addiction works: in order to get the same result, you need more... Something new is only new the first time you see it. The second time, it is not new, less interesting, because it's already known, seen, experienced. No judgment, no comparison. I know there is more than just visual effects. And an experience is only as good as we truly experience it and when it presents itself in the "now" versus spending a huge amount of mental energy, to compare it with something from the past and take us away from experiencing the moment in other ways, such as thinking, thinking, thinking. This time I do an experiment and ask a question. The other people had asked questions to "Mother Ayahuasca" and received answers. I had not asked questions before. I was open to explore whatever would show up. But this time I will. For me, there is no Mother Ayahuasca. From me, that knowledge, that we access during the ceremony, that they call Mother Ayahuasca, is part of my own consciousness, which in my perception is part of one big pot of energy, all there is. The plant "gets" us there, by altering and extending our minds. That's how I can access it. It is there anyway, I just don't realize it during regular states of awareness with a half unconscious, habitual mindset. It is

6 - Third Ayahuasca Night

nothing external, I am part of it. Clearly! It doesn't really matter how you call that phenomenon, words are just limiting, trying to use boxes to understand the organization of life.

So the question today is: What is my job, my duty on earth? A job description, please!

Immediately I hear "stories." So I keep asking "write stories?" Hear "participate in stories." What does that mean? Can be acting. Can be storytelling, which I did already a lot in coaching. Can mean simply living, creating those stories every day. Am I supposed to bring "my own flavor" to the stories, participate in them and share? Not quite a job description but certainly interesting. Am trusting that the full meaning of the "story" answer will drop in, all by itself when the time is right.

That night I walk home by myself. I take all the time I need to get back on my feet. I take all the time I need to guide myself down the staircase. I take breaks to look at the sky and enjoy the jungle at night. I focus on the walk, exactly how I teach coaching clients: stop trying to get somewhere without experiencing the walk.

The first Ayahuasca nights I felt eager to get into bed. Uncomfortable with that unknown state of experiencing. Now, I surrender. A new mindset, no fighting the discomfort and just going with what is. A totally different experience. This night, I no longer judge how I feel, good or bad, what I want, or what I don't want. Still, the experience at night after the ceremony is just as unpleasant, but I am OK with all there is. I no longer suffered from it.

* * *

The next day, as I had already experienced before, the bits and pieces of information dropped together and I could understand the meaning of the ceremony. Stories.

Coming to Majorca with my kids in 2003, I had been invited to a model agency's Christmas party. The kids had been modeling for their dad's new wife's business in Ibiza and therefore were listed with that agency. Since we didn't know anybody on the island, we decided to go to the party and meet some new people. At the end, I was asked to join the agency, which I did. Why not? Take it as a hobby and learn something new ... Soon after, I had my first job as a thirty-eight-year-old senior model. It was an interesting experience. I had never done any performing or stage work, nor been on focus. At least not that I knew of. I doubted if I would be pretty enough and physically in good-enough shape, able to do posing or even walk on heels. The old doubt. My first job was a shooting at a golf course with an experienced actor. No clue of golf nor modeling, I improvised and had a heck of a time. That was the beginning. Then I did many jobs thereafter. What totally thrilled me were leading parts in TV commercials. Since I am one of a kind, not like everybody else, my kind was booked for a specific type of job only. Always fun stuff or moving emotions! After the fifth TV commercial I wondered what it would be like to check out acting. The mere thought to go into acting already stressed me out. That's an insane thought, I judged. At forty-plus, no official acting training, no experience, no connections. Is that some kind of suppressed vanity coming out now?

One day, I found myself sitting in the plane to LA, listening to my inner dialogue: if somebody asked me whether I wanted to participate in a movie as an actress, and if it was my kind of thing, inspiring, positive, clean, not too much of a challenge, in terms of how much text I had to learn or what I had to do, and if it paid at least the trip getting there, then, I would not say no ...

How complicated! Instead of just allowing to go for it, without doubt.

Only a few weeks after that flight one of my modeling agents from Mallorca sent me an inquiry for a movie. I didn't even have to go to a casting. The job was a small role in a German TV movie and paid just enough to cover the traveling costs. That was my first acting gig. I loved it. I loved the interaction with the team, the teamwork and the personal connections during a "workday" during the breaks as well as the "safe" way of expressing emotions in front of the camera.

And at the same time I, or probably my rational mind, was confused what was going on. Scared on a subtle level that being an actress was somehow unacceptable. Later, I asked myself what that meant, really: unacceptable. Unacceptable by whom if not me? Why not sneak into a totally different field, after managing director, seminar organizer and coach? Why limit myself?

6 - Third Ayahuasca Night

I loved to understand how other people feel in their skins. Why not interpret those "fake" situations the way I would? I was a very empathetic person and had worked with hundreds of clients as a coach getting to know almost everything about them. So acting resulted very easy for me.

That night in the jungle, I got the message that my job is to share stories. Stories help to expand the box, to dare to look beyond limitations, to sneak into a world that is unknown for you and simply by looking into it, you can't make it unseen, you can't deny it any longer what you have seen, and the person in the story could be you. That's the whole point about stories. We identify with the protagonist, fearlessly, without limiting beliefs or walls. That's why fairy tales work or stories in hypnotherapy the way Milton Erickson told them.

* * *

It felt like, I gave myself permission to do what I like to do. Or Mother Ayahuasca did it for me, haha.

The next day, I felt at ease, even though the mind was busy all night like every other night after ceremony. I did not sleep. The local mind was trying to figure out stuff. It's okay, I said to myself. Everybody else seemed to experience more feelings. I experienced mostly pictures and then insights dropped down out of the blue, shortly after, without me pondering about the meaning. It just came.

I also wanted to experience feelings during ceremony. Something "real," related to life in a body. But I did not get any, just no body experiences. Feeling is connected to the body. Sensations are connected to the body. My experiences were mind-blowingly spiritual.

I figured I would ask for feelings next time. I mean, ask to explore what feelings are about, experience them in ceremony, gain insights, what they are for, really. I mean there is basically one pleasant feeling, that of joy, and three "ugly" one's, anger, fear, sadness. At least that is what my judgmental thinking concluded. 25% fun, the rest drag. Is that correct?

I did have experiences of awe and peace and total surrender, surrendering the body, letting go of control, freedom! The local mind shut up, allowing the process to unfold.

No experience of anger, fear, sadness, joy so far. What happened there? If all the programming of the local mind was shut off, in order to access the big mind, the one field, then the other mundane human feelings were just not there. I had been familiar with my local mind so far only. The local mind in my understanding at the time was like that part of nonphysical reality, where rational thinking happens. It also is where irrational thinking happens, without us being aware of it. There conditioning is managing the process, that's what made me unconsciously judge myself to never feel good enough. Moral. Dogmas. Unreal stuff. Have to's. Obligations. Duties. Drag. That what gives us a hard time, even when there is no hard time.

That what wants to know, and is not ok with just knowing. It also wants to know the reason behind the knowledge, to make sure it is true, to prove why you know what you know. Evidence is not good enough. The scientific mind wants proof. Despite placebo. Despite knowing that things can work just because you believe in them, and using the placebo effect in some cases, it's like not accepting it really. Doing scientific research, to then ten years later find out that what you researched was a very limited vision of what is really going on. And then, nineteen years later, there is no more value to these studies. In fact, they may become irrelevant. In "reality" the earth is not a disk, and many drugs don't help, they merely reduce the perception of the pain and create a huge market …

My "small" childish mind wanted to make sure to do the right thing, stay in control, so nothing bad would happen. What a funny idea anyway. That made it so hard to let go, relax and especially to trust.

What if I had already worked out how to release and let go of ego? Scary! Can ego be all gone, ever? Is that enlightenment? Does it stay? Is that illusion of thinking that you know separating you from the rest of the co-earth's inhabitants and creation? Prevent us from experiencing oneness? Confusing …

What if I am that perfect something of creation already, even if I don't know that I am, already? No need to work hard on myself any longer? Wow!

6 - Third Ayahuasca Night

"But" ... the small mind screams, how will I know? Do I know that I have permission to just trust? Who gives me permission and why?

Blah blah blah.

7 - New Year's in the Amazon

Ending the Year with Insights

Journal Entry
31.12.2014

Last day of the year. In the middle of the Amazon rain forest, far away from "civilization."

Today is a peaceful day. After the last Ayahuasca night I feel more relaxed. That work requires quite some energy. Some part of me is processing all night. I'm listening to an amazing tropical rain, like a huge orchestra, playing for me. Vast and loud. I feel blessed. Today is the first day in the jungle that I am strong enough to do yoga. My German Peruvian friend, the first guy I met in Iquitos when I first arrived, left. He had only come for a few days to experiment with Ayahuasca. He has a big heart.

Today, I had a conflict with one of the managers. She was overwhelmed and broke down in tears. She felt my teaching was too demanding and asked for traditional ways to learning languages. I wondered what would be the worst-case scenario of this situation and immediately stayed in control of my emotions, appropriate to the situation, observing the mechanism of emotions running the situation. I realized that my emotions were adequate to the situation. No automatic habitual reaction. Just the truth. Something has shifted. I remember how I would have usually reacted when being criticized directly, especially in this situation, in the jungle, taking hallucinogenic drugs.

There was some memory of how my habitual reaction would look like, but it did not occur. I was in control without controlling. Amazing. This is what I ask for in any situation

7 - New Year's in the Amazon

from now on. I can allow my response with grace and humbleness. I don't need to ponder over possible consequences. Just stay truthful to myself. This kind of clarity, courage and determination to be truthful to myself, I will also ask for when it comes to close relationships. I realized I had been holding back my truth out of fear of emotional reactions and therefore did not show up as I truly am. For the poor excuse to make sure I was not hurting anybody.

Thinking of my friend the Do-gooder, the YouTube video promoter, the one who showed me that video, that started all this. I feel detached and yet connected. This guy could use some good healing vibrations as well, so I sent him some, without any personal ideas of what I might think he would need for healing. Like a wish or a prayer. Put out the intention without worrying about how it should or will happen. Let go and let it happen, trust.

The right thing happens at the right time as long as I get out of the way or as long as ego gets out of the way.

I have been talking about my past marriage with one of the managers. She has been in high distress. I shared some of my experiences. Decided to no longer talk much about the past. Only if it is necessary, really important or beneficial.

Objective: be good to yourself! Notice how many of us are very hard on ourselves. I have been very hard on myself without ever realizing it at all. No longer!

- Appreciate what is, now.
- Transform by reading the truth, instead of judging. This is how you let go of suffering.
- Act according to the best for all—unity, not just personal preferences, this includes what is best for you to start out with.
- See the very big picture!

Feeling a happy new year coming up next with lots of joy, love, expansion, abundance, growth, peace and harmony.

Headless Chicken

What am I looking for in Ayahuasca? I wasn't looking for Ayahuasca to start out with, but I was following a calling. So my mind was not requesting, my soul was. Now, my mind wants to know why. I now know: I want to learn to live my soul purpose and clearly distinguish between the truth and ego stuff.

Before I had always doubted whether my ego was manipulating the truth; in other words, was I listening to programmed monkey mind chatter or was that the truth that I was hearing? In fact, during my first experiences in the jungle it looked like I already knew all that stuff, I just didn't trust I did. I doubted myself, my intuition, my deep-down knowing: I had been trained to accept what I got taught instead of learning how to listen inside and how to find out for myself instead of taking on other's subjective viewpoints.

At this point I still want to make sure no ego sneaks in and fades the truth! I do have questions as well: in sexuality and other aspects of enjoyment I still seem to hold back—ego working. What is the purpose of that? Protection? How can I stop that, stop holding back, allowing to let go, letting go of deep-down fears? Ayahuasca? Change my mind? Change my brain structure to overwrite that very old program of "you must not" and "shame on you," and "you should feel bad about yourself!"

I know that I can't change by thinking and accumulating information, but by experiencing something new. In "real life" it is about breaking the habit of automatic reactions. I happened to meet my YouTube friend to help me with that, he came to me for that, and he knew. I came to him to open him up for the idea of something else I had been exploring: acceptance and being okay with what is, instead of fighting. Instead of fighting, choosing new responses to a situation. I had not quite mastered that virtue. In my past, I tried to accept, be okay, not fight and then resign. That was not a solution. I needed to speak up for myself, live my truth, instead of fighting others or resigning.

With help of Ayahuasca I can continue what I had been working on for so many years: work my way through the busy mind, use it, not be used by it. Serenity. What was new was that I could learn to make friends with that part inside of myself that was bugging me, sabotaging me. Accept my shadows, include them, bring them to the light, transcend them by becoming more forgiving to myself. Stop

7 - New Year's in the Amazon

putting myself down unconsciously and being hard on myself. José the shaman says 50% of what you see in Ayahuasca is true and 50% of what you see is testing you, so you become stronger. Sounds like martial arts philosophy. He referred to a couple who had seen during Ayahuasca trips that they should separate and follow different routes. I took that 50/50 advice seriously and contemplated. I had seen a lot already. What he says doesn't mean to wipe out the 50% you don't like, but to look for a deeper meaning of those pictures. So instead of taking each picture or story you have been seeing during Ayahuasca ceremony and acting upon it in the material world, you first need to focus on your personal big picture, what major issue has been going on in your life, translate it, not get distracted. For those two it meant, instead of separating right away, they might ask themselves what is truly important for each of them, individually and in this relationship. And be honest. Then you might come to the conclusion that there is no more growth and a joint pathway for those two beings and it is okay to separate without drama. Yet, just separating without getting the point will make you just repeat the same drama in the next relationship. It is about being honest with yourself. Acting upon something just because "Mother Ayahuasca" has told you is missing the whole point of living your truth. Question it, what does it mean for you? Really? At least 50% is just to test your ego or truth, according to Don José.

My personal goal is to inspire others in big and small ways. I do that by living an inspired life myself, focused on love rather than hatred or fear, focus on solutions rather than problems, live a healthy lifestyle. Instead of distracting the mind and the body, sharpening the saw. I simply want to live a good life, learn, inspire and share with others. I want to live as an individual, connected to something bigger than myself.

My objective is to live my best, bring out my best, use it for the service of the big picture, with a loving, sexy partner, enjoying the pathway, open to accept and give in abundance. Even though I have no clue how to do that exactly. All I know is that there is no job description. I need to find out myself by experimenting. Trusting that what I feel is what I feel is what some part of myself wants me to listen to and that part guides me to the next crossing.

8 - Ayahuasca Trip 4

Why Things Are Changing

In the mornings, sitting at the long breakfast table anytime between 10 and 1 PM we all meet, communicate and share. I noticed how easy it is to get influenced by other people's vibrations, ideas and impact. I felt that before, but now it was very obvious. Believing that it is most important for every human being to be themselves less of a product of copying others unconsciously, I decided to talk and share less of my experiences. Unless I felt it was really important or necessary to help people open up their minds for possibilities out there, beyond what they know, how one can experience a situation. We are so little aware of the power of our thoughts and especially of our words. Me too, even though I work on it. In those three months in the jungle I could clearly see the impact of thoughts and words on ourselves and others. One word cannot really mess up somebody, unless that somebody accepts it. That is exactly the point: most of the time we are in a habitual state of limited awareness, some kind of automatic reaction state where we just take on whatever comes toward us, whether we want it or not. And then, that affects unwanted consequences. Not being aware of this process, we then believe that other people did that to us, instead of acknowledging our lack of awareness and freedom to reject and say No to what doesn't fit for us.

Journal Entry
January 2, 2015

That night I see fewer pictures during Ayahuasca, have fewer thoughts, nothing pretty or ugly, no judgments at all, it just is. Interesting. Am in a state of awe, not comfortable not uncomfortable. Bizarre. Body and surroundings is one, my body is part of the picture, while I am aware of being in the

8 - Ayahuasca Trip 4

body. Warmth enters hands and feet, solar plexus and heart and breast area.

"Your hands are your power—Power is in your hands!" I can act, use my hands. Yes, it is the mind that directs power into the hands. It is Self-directed energy, giving power to the hands, therefore we have the mind. The mind is the link from spiritual to physical world experience, from soul to body.

I feel a strong pain in the abdomen. Ouch. Very strong. Feels like labor, giving birth to a baby. Thank God I already know how that feels and there is no need to panic. Whatever it is that I feel, it is so painful that I bite my hand. Yet, it is okay. Just pain. I see a brown thing, like a dried-up embryo in my belly, like a gigantic brown bean. And me giving birth to it. It's me! That thing in my belly is me. Very very painful. I gave birth to myself. Weird. Very weird. As if I hadn't been born yet, or the body was born, but the soul just didn't want to stay in it. This time, it is very clearly my own choice to be born. No blaming to be born in the wrong environment or something. I did it, I chose, whereas before, I always doubted that I really would have chosen this life, my personal experience in this body and in these circumstances voluntarily, ha ha. I can see clearly now. I can see that everything makes sense, even when the logical mind is way too limited to see and understand the whole picture. I can allow myself to let go of trying to understand everything with the logical mind. I can sit back, relax and allow to tap into a deeper state of being and experiencing life and myself. When I don't do that and the monkey mind is too loud to hear my real voice, I immediately notice, because it feels like suffering. Whenever I don't understand something, or things work out differently than I thought they would, it kind of hurts. It could be that easy to let go of suffering?!

As I go home in the middle of the night, strong rain started. Feel my body all tight and tense. Had been tense before, after the other ceremonies already, but this time, I was just more aware of the tension in the body. Then, I hear my own loud voice telling myself: "It's okay, you're in the body. It's okay." Like a mantra. Very weird and at the same time not weird at all. Soul having a human experience. Changing perspectives, expanding perspectives and understanding.

Again I have a long night, the mind is disturbed, at least that part of the mind I am used to. Wild, searching for something, searching for relief, peace, love, caressing, comfort, unity. Oh yes: during Ayahuasca ceremony I asked: why do I see what I see? What is the reason for that show of shapes and movements of limitless creativity? The answer is: for joy, for entertainment purely!

Really? Just for joy? Is that enough? Doesn't there have to be a more severe, sincere reason? Something hard, something meaningful, something to do with survival or fighting? Whatever!

The place I come from is full of joy and entertainment, ease, flow, nonduality. Where I live now, the place I live in the body, is confrontational and conflictive. Constantly, I need to respond, make decisions, face conflicts. The unity seems to be gone, replaced by conflicts and friction.

At the moment I wonder if the show I see is in the spiritual world. But somehow I have a feeling it is just the opposite: What I see in the ceremony is "real." The show is in the physical world, and what is really true, is the spiritual world. Can we separate it anyway?

All I know so far is that it is special to be born, because we get to play in the show. That's why I am here. To play, enjoy, create stories. We create drama, friction, tension, ups and downs and make sure it never gets boring. And if it gets boring, we just create some kind of experience that makes us want to change or forces us to do so. There is a lot of strong tinting in "life": feelings.

Oh, I asked another question: who would be the ideal guy for me, should I ever consider to get into a relationship again? I see some kind of Tarzan. Oh no, I thought to myself. No American actor. No ego drama. But I certainly like Tarzan, the one from the story.

7 - A New Start

I Am No Longer That What I Thought I Was

The heavy rains force us to wear rain boots again to cross the puddles of mud in the jungle. It is very humid and sticky. Even my backpack starts building mold. Every day I witness natural spectacles in the rain forest. The sounds are magical. It feels like you could hear thousands of sounds. I can sense the energy. It is cleansing and liberating. There is no more doubt that some kind of super boredom or cravings for Western luxuries could harm my experiences during these months to come yet. I am confident and trust that I am all safe. Saying that doesn't mean that I had no moments of being bored or fancied a good beer or a bathtub or meeting up with some friends. I also was wondering how my kids were doing. But now I knew that I no longer suffered from those moments. I could just accept and trust and allow things to fall into place, the way they fall into place. That was a brand-new experience. No need to worry, plan, control. I had always felt I needed to make sure that everything went right. Fear in the neck. Obviously, it is absurd and arrogant to think I could control the world. It doesn't make any sense either. If everybody would be able to do so, it would be a big mess. And it is! The real problem is that we do not recognize our own power to create our own experiences. We create without knowing, unconsciously. Plus, we try and fight reality and what it is, we don't want or didn't expect though, even well-meant, consciously or not, to manipulate others! That prevents us from enjoying the experience of now fully and creates a constant struggle. So now I can no longer act as if I had to make sure everything worked out fine for everybody and therefore stress myself out. That was nothing more than a mere excuse and distraction to live up to my real potential. Focus on what's wrong, instead of living your life, doing what you came here for. And that what I came here for was still to be found out. I only knew I came to play, communicate and inspire. And the play was the part that was most difficult to accept. Play? Just play and have a good time? Really? Is that "enough?" Well, honestly, it doesn't sound too bad, after all. If there is a God, he sure wants us to enjoy ourselves and each other.

All I knew at that point was that I could not limit myself to the thinking mind. Nor could I complain to be a victim of strong emotions that showed up as a consequence of something that was triggering some kind of a button inside of me. Yes, that seems to be the way my system was programmed, but that's not me. I know I no longer can excuse my own power to stay asleep and allow this to happen.

All it took was a little bit of self-awareness and honesty. Looking at myself from a wider perspective. Seeing the whole picture, instead of continuing to limit my view and my experiences to what I had known and experienced before. It is just like looking through the keyhole and seeing to the other side. There, I always see the same restricted scene. But now, I not only know that there is not even a door that could restrict my perspective, I also know that restricting my experience to seeing, hearing, and feeling with yesterday's senses and programs meant really to play the old record, instead of becoming aware of what really is, here and now. How could I maintain this knowledge in every day's life and every day's awareness? As soon as habitual thinking took over, which was most of the time, I lost the thread. What would be the key to stay in this state of higher awareness? I don't see the point of spending a lifetime like a monk, practicing yoga, tai chi or meditation all day long in order to raise consciousness. I have a clear feeling that I have lived such a monk-type life before, it's not on my list of things to learn. This time around it is about bringing that spiritual consciousness into every day's life. Also, for me it was not an option to become a shaman or continue with medicinal plants for the rest of my life. I can just feel that this is not for me this time around. It is not my purpose. I do believe there are people out there who strongly feel this to be their purpose, and that's okay. It's not me. I can no longer deny what I clearly feel and what I clearly do not feel.

That evening I go to ceremony with this strange feeling. I still wonder if my ego wants to play with me and hold me back from exploring deeper and more. Was it the ego tricking me to manipulate my decisions and to stay in control? That night I felt sick without even taking Ayahuasca. I go over to the ceremony and decide to go back and not participate. Something said no. Clearly. I still went over to the ceremony hall to talk to the shamans. They told me to trust my gut and sent me home. I took a break. I sing fifty-four Maha Mrityunjaya

9 - A New Start

mantras and go to sleep. I relax the body and digest all the experiences. In the morning I wake up with a feeling of expansion in the heart area. Yes!!!

This is exactly the vibration I want to be in all the time. Hadn't felt it in a while. Last time hugging some friends goodbye. Then, I was so busy searching that I did not feel at all. All mind. No more connection. No more relation.

My conclusion that day: Rule number one: trust your guts. Guts are smarter than the thinking brain, because they feel out of the box. Brain only knows out of the box stuff when it is in a special state such as alpha, theta or delta or so. In regular thinking modes it only refers to the information stored from the past and dreams, which is inaccurate information, because it is not present. It may be subconscious stuff that fades the picture. That might need to be translated and understood. What does that really mean? Like Ayahuasca: the shamans said you can't take it all as a direct answer. 50% of the messages or pictures is challenging you and you need to look deeper to understand. It is like when you dream and wake up, you might remember a dream thinking to yourself: how weird. Then, later, either somebody else triggers it or it falls from heaven into your mind and it clicks: I got it! That means ... This is one way, how we get to clear out the stuff "under the carpet." Pictures come up to look at some issue now, from a safe distance. An issue that you are now ready and safe to look at and to let go of. Something that you had suppressed or forgotten because you couldn't deal with it at the time.

We need to focus on the guts when thinking, feeling or taking decisions. The belly, the tan tien, the core. Some scientists call it the bigger brain, because it is so sophisticated in its way of operating. And I am not only referring to digesting "material" food ...

Insight: the soul is the link merging with all, with spirit and with the three-dimensional world of time and space. All is moving around, observing, nothing but enjoying entertainment or call it experiences, like being or participating in an amazing spectacle of boundless creativity. Visual science fiction in every day's life: always new pictures, different shapes and movements, never ever boring to watch and merge with. For the sake of joy. No conflict, no doubt, no duality, no fight, harmoniously moving together, like a constantly evolving structure.

Headless Chicken

Healing the soul means something like letting go of restrictions, pain, unforgiven anger, judgment, ego, having to be right or better.

After "giving birth to myself" during the last Ayahuasca ceremony I can see clearly: pain exists in the body. Physical pain. And suffering only happens in the mind. Suffering is produced by judging a situation, e.g. reading the pain as painful and focusing on it. Mental focus on something else than the current pain results in no suffering. The soul can evolve by incarnating in a body and then in this "position" realize itself, what it really is about, its powers, its limitless possibilities of choosing whatever it wishes. The human experience allows the soul to experience body and mind and evolve on this level by healing, expanding and overcoming limitations. Therefore, the human state is a unique gift where we can experiment, expand, create, transform, enjoy. And if we raise our consciousness, we can overcome former limitations and become the creators we are. The soul doesn't judge. The mind judges and creates suffering. Yet, the soul had the purpose to incarnate in this body. And each of us has the job to find out for themselves. It is of no use to copy teachers, books or philosophies. Cognitive processes are not effective when it comes to finding out what we are here for. That state of peace or love or bliss is not over-exaggerated enthusiasm or high-pitch feelings, nor the manic depressive state, it is beyond feelings. The home base is on another ground. It is not a state of feeling and emotion, rather a state of being. Being in a positive state—that's about it. Peace, calmness, tranquility, can be pretty unspectacular for a judging mind that is conditioned to follow trends like a sheep. Or it can be the last or only hope for someone who is desperate to find meaning in his or her existence. The ability to enjoy.

That other state of consciousness using Ayahuasca medicine in a way helped me to mentally understand and remember that "feeling" which is not really an emotion, more an experience, a state of being, a state of being in awe, being awe. No difference between me and awe. When I wrote that in my diary, I had to look up what the word awe really meant, because I had not heard of that word before. For some reason I wrote my experiences in the English language even though I lived in Spain, was in Peru, and my mother tongue was German. I suppose bliss is another verbal expression for what I referred to and it is the same thing in any country, no matter how you call it.

9 - A New Start

Giving birth is painful for both, the one giving birth and the newborn. I now have the chance to look at the world in a brand-new way, interact and participate freely, fearlessly, free of judgments, concepts and programming. I can distinguish between truth and manipulating thinking processes, between acting from compassion and manipulating. Acting from a place of love or out of fear. I can choose what I want. I see what is right or wrong for me in that moment, without judging others, just choosing for myself. Trusting my guts. I can share my experience with people who come and search for answers, people who have lost faith, hope, vision, heart-connection. My heart is waking up again. Some time ago outside influences and the chatter of my mind were numbing the heart.

Giving birth to a body is the way to manifest in the material world. With or without body, the soul is connected with all, like an interactive network. In that sense the earth is like a playground for the soul where it can not only heal, but build or play whatever it wants.

What does it want? How do you know what the soul really wants?

I never wanted much. No wishes, no disappointments, I thought. But that was tricking myself, thinking wishes away, and not being truthful. I also had wishes, but I doubted if that wish came from my true self or from my ego mind. Now it sounds so simple: whatever idea, wish, dream, plan, vision makes the heart beat higher is what the soul wants. When the person is totally polluted by education, manipulative programming from others, who want to take advantage of a person for their own use and benefit, drugs, bad influences, an egotistical me, me, me mindset, or having lost contact and connection to the heart, then they can't hear the soul's message. In such a state of obsessive thinking, addiction or feeling lost, a person is driven by cravings and fears. Disconnected. Constantly distracting, never in real connection, relating to oneself and others, suppressing real needs. Depression is when a human being shuts down true connection due to frustration, fear of rejection or conflict, resignation, giving up hope, seeing no light, no direction, no reason to live at all. This person is stuck in the mind which disconnects from heart. Feelings seem dangerous for that person, negative feelings at least. No feelings, no joy, no enjoyment. Overwhelmed by negative thoughts, without even being aware of them, disconnected from feelings that person obviously can't listen to the heart. How can he or she possibly follow the soul path then, instead of following other sheep? He or she needs healing. Pills prevent them from committing suicide, but don't heal. That's what Ayahuasca medicine can do. And yet, it is just a helper. I firmly believe we have access to our healing powers by raising consciousness only. All I learned in the jungle in those months came to me like a confirmation of something that I already knew, that was already there in the field of consciousness. That I knew already, showed the first few pages in my diary, that I wrote like hypnotic writing, it just came out of me without passing the thinking mind. We know, once we get out of our own way.

As I lie in bed at night I hear and see myself giving a talk to many people. Like a movie or a dream that I create and am conscious about. I remember the vision of that dream, ten years ago, it was déjà-vu. I am a newborn child, free to do whatever makes my heart beat higher. Free to discover pleasures of the body, free to act, play in movies, play in that show, dance, sing, give seminars, play more, travel, interview people, anything I want. I always had that choice. I just didn't realize, didn't know because I didn't remember. And I don't have to do anything. I just know that I may if I wish so. Nothing can stop me. I had this dream of giving a talk to many people before at nighttime years ago, it was not a daydream. This time I don't doubt it was okay to want those things. Now, I know I can do this. Why not? It is about daring to dream, daring to choose and going for it, even though you don't know exactly how yet. It is about letting the monkey mind criticize or intimidate without giving it too much attention. Let it play its games, while you stick to what is really important for you.

Life energy is blocked when disconnected from the soul. When you don't feel yourself anymore. When you do things you don't really want to do and you know they are not good for you but somehow, you don't have the energy to change that freaking habit. That's when you are a slave of some kind, of a virus in the mind.

It is not food, drinks and air that keeps us alive only. It is some kind of individual life spark that ignites the light in the body and mind every day. A current that runs in the veins that is not just blood. An energy behind everything.

I always thought depression is a disease of the mind, like uncontrollable negative thinking habits. But this is just the consequence, not the

9 - A New Start

cause. The source of the problem to be cured is the connection to the soul. This connection can't be maintained with mental thinking processes. Obsessive positive thinking habits act like antidepressants, band-aids over and over again. How exhausting. There is no flow in this approach. It does not heal the original cause of the disease. Only by reconnecting to the source we come from can we become compassionate for that little being in the body, ourselves. The body and mind is just an expression of the soul, temporarily incarnated, here to act. It is our tool, our play-dough, our puppet to play with, interact with others, direct and be good to, love like a puppy. The special thing about this body device is that it can feel. Like a thermostat, feelings indicate exactly what the situation is. We need to keep that system clean so energy can flow. All the stuff that has accumulated in our system from ancestors, upbringing, conditioning is not ours. We need to cleanse that. That is what healing is about. Make the original self whole again. Heal it from scars. That is the difference between higher Self and lower self. The true you and the program that is running in the monkey mind keeping you from experiencing the here and now. Feeling yourself in this very moment instead of triggering the autopilot to replay old emotions keeping us from free will and choice. The true you is felt here and now, not thought. It is not emotional replay of some past experience. It is felt. It feels loving and peaceful. It is not imagined and visualized. All that stuff that is going on when thinking, evaluating, judging, expecting, interpreting, blah blah blah is activity of the thinking mind, the monkey mind, not of the true self. Knowing this is not enough, but you must also experience, feeling this soul-being, feeling that energy, that is part of all energy, "the force." Then we can allow ourselves to focus and relax into meditation and look at the situation from soul level. Like looking from the other side, the higher big perspective. Observing from there, we can just smile and be OK with ourselves, remember who we really are beyond the physical facade and mental software. Exhale, accept what is, play with the scene, response from the heart, remember who we are.

Long talk with Don José, the shaman. "You are here to enjoy. Nothing more than that." That's exactly what I got out of the ceremonies. But for some reason my rational mind doesn't want to believe it. Other people get other messages and have different steps to go on their paths. I am here to enjoy the jungle, the river, the birds, the people… Interesting. Conclusion of the day: let go of doubt and enjoy, no more questioning whether it's okay to just enjoy. Let that monkey in the mind play, don't attempt to kill it. Just remember you are not the monkey mind. Change perspective.

Jan 3, 4 PM: Fire ceremony

The shamans and helpers were brewing a new batch of Ayahuasca. There is a special location for the brewing next to "El Centro," the central high-ceiling two-story wooden building where we meet to eat, exchange, hang out in hammocks, read or talk to the shamans. Close to the center is a special area, a plain ground without plants with three fireplaces. There are three huge pots on top of the open wood fires. They are filled with a layer of Chacruna leaves, a layer of peeled and shredded Ayahuasca vines, a layer of leaves, another layer of vines and so on. Peeling the vines was a job for three or four men during many hours. Preparing the broth will take another eight hours. Out of each huge pot they cook approximately three liters of Ayahuasca. Once the brew is finished, the fire ceremony ritual follows.

The fire ceremony is part of the Ayahuasca experience in the Healing Retreat Center. The purpose of this special event is to clean out what no longer suits you, get rid of stuff that bugged you in the past, things that carry negative energy, memories, traits, habits.

Each of us projects our negative thoughts, feelings and habits onto an object that is supposed to be burnt in the fire. To make it easier, we write down anything we want to get rid of on a piece of paper and wrap it around a burnable object such as a little branch of a tree. One after one, we step forward to Don José, who starts the ceremony by protecting us with smoke of a burning stick and sprays aguafuerte all over us, so the protection would last, he says. We shall never forget that day and the liberation from any negativity. Emptying out negativity doesn't mean that exposure to new negative energy won't have an impact. It still does. What definitely lasted was the realization that negativity is a choice. Being an empath, at times I feel others' feelings more than my own. It took another year or so of discipline and practice to stop being mad at myself for picking up negative energy from others. I had not conquered my ego after Ayahuasca, even after the fire ceremony. But I became aware of what is mine and what is not. What is real. What is now. What I am. I remember getting mad when exposed to people's egos. When they know everything already, no matter what topic comes

9 - A New Start

up. When the cup is so full that nothing else fits inside and you better not even get in touch, to not upset their full cup. When information is stored to the top of their being and there is no room for experiencing. I became annoyed. First at them, then at myself for getting annoyed. Annoyed and annoyed again. Angry. Then, I just observed and let go of judging. All of the sudden, the struggle was gone. I could just be and let them be. Let us be.

I was wondering how the depressed girl was experiencing this event. It had not been her first fire ceremony, since she had been at the retreat center quite some time already. Was there any hope left? The idea is to rid yourself of negativity ...

I was contemplating about the type of inner conflict she might have. Almost giving up hope, feeling offended when someone tells her she looked better, since they "had no clue how she felt inside" and still going to fire ceremony. She seemed to be stuck in feeling bad in one way or another forever, convinced that nobody could help her. At the same time she came back to doing Ayahuasca for a second time, another month intensively up to five times a week in her despair. To me it was like ego screaming: I am not giving up control! No matter how many ceremonies, how good you look, I am not letting go, I won't trust anybody, anything. I can keep you in my hands simply by giving you a hard time to be present. I will let your hard-wired memories rule over your life.

She identified with her thought-emotions roller coaster.

I experienced that tendency toward a generally rather negative state of mind/emotion can be caused by an incident, such as a loss of a loved one or separation or disease. Most of the time, however, I observed that not the incident of the past as such, but the tendency to ponder over it, judge it, criticize the system or situation, or simply fear of feeling low would cause these almost unbearable feelings. So for me it was the thought that fed the emotion. And the emotion was like an explanation or an excuse for the annoying thoughts. And so the spiral continued going down. Some people say it is due to the nature of the human mind to protect himself, to forecast worst-case scenarios, in order to be prepared. A survival thing. Ego is supposed to help survive originally. That would mean that anyone has rather a tendency to negativity than to positivity even without a very traumatizing experience. Human nature is to see the dark as a survival tool. Interestingly, in "undeveloped" countries, there seems to be hardly any depression. There material growth or making money to add more "wealth" in form of stuff into their lives is not so important. The main focus of people's attention is having enough to eat. Don't these humans have a tendency for negativity, a mechanism to secure survival there?

My subjective observation is, they don't ponder, criticize or judge so much. They can be present, less in the mind, more in the body, here and now, present with their hearts as well. They seem to be busier with living than with thinking. They do more, they act. They don't just act to distract, not having to feel or feel good about themselves. They just do what has to be done, without judging, without pondering if they like or dislike what they do all the time. And they are faster to quit what they don't like or what they feel is not right for them; it seems they have less fear of the future. Do they have a different type of ego? Referring to ego as that part of the mind that mediates between the conscious and the unconscious and that is responsible for reality testing and a sense of personal identity. Are they more open to reality, change and more aware to the meaning of their lives?

If there is a thought-cause and emotion-effect equation, vice versa, would that mean that the ego that wants to be right and in control all the time is the main driver of depression by suppressing real feelings and living in thoughts only, busy mediating conscious and unconscious? Can that program running called ego possibly construct our own prison by building neuronal connections according to what we think about ourselves? Can this idea of who we think we are keep us trapped in ego-walls with a foundation of thought patterns that we never truly questioned, that are possibly not really ours to start out with? And then hormones functioning like glue to that virtual construction of our perception of ourselves and our reality? Gosh, how fake, and effective in a negative way …

When that spiral has been going on for a long time, people stop "forcing" themselves to cut the vicious cycle of negative thought patterns or burning out running behind external goals without ever finding the true meaning of their lives. They stop making an effort to change for good, do something good for themselves, such as going outdoors, spending time in nature and natural daylight or some kind

9 - A New Start

of an action that involves other people and cooperation. They reduce themselves to super-functional and the hormones go crazy to indicate something is off balance here.

Then there is such a thing as fear of depression. Having had depressions, you are left with the memory of dark times and the consequences of those dark times. I have a feeling that fear of depression is somehow a bigger issue in terms of numbers of people suffering from it than depression. It happens so often. Better not be too joyful, your mood might change and resent in a minute to have indulged the other side of the coin. And the contrast from joy to low is even worse than feeling discontent to feeling really low.

It works just like fear. How many times were we in fear, and how many times did the situation we were afraid of actually happen, other than in our imagination? Like a nightmare. You can have it over and over again without anything ever actually happening. Same with fear and fear of depression.

With that depressed girl, I had come to the conclusion to not get involved too much since she did not appreciate it, but got angry if anybody showed interest in trying to support her. On the other hand, she was craving attention. My learning assignment was to let go of trying to manipulate certain situations in any way, positively or negatively, but be myself. What that "myself" really meant for me, I had to define myself. I had to question that, feel what filled my heart, explore the meaning behind. And quite possibly I had to clear out the ideas and habits that didn't fit to who I really wanted to be from now on. Change the way I thought about myself. Become, or be the me I want to be, the me I came here for to be.

10 - Ayahuasca Trip 5

Unexpected Healing

Francisco, the other shaman, visited me almost every day. He put some herbal stuff on my chest that was blocked, to release mucus. He also enjoyed talking with me, exchanging and hanging out. And so did I. I love to learn about people. Who they really are. What moves their hearts. What are their dreams, their priorities, their values and beliefs. One day he came and needed money to send to his brother. He said his brother had an accident and was in jail right now, and he needed to send him money to bail him out. I lent him some money, even though I had not much cash left and no way to get cash. But I didn't need much anyway. Shortly after, the managers tell me that he frequently had some issue going on where he needed money. They would not lend him any money. That was the managers' story. Instead of freaking out, I decided to focus on getting the money back.

Considering how little money they are paid compared to us Westerners and hanging out with Western people all the time, I understand when all of a sudden what was good enough before is no longer good enough. I was on a work exchange and didn't make any money for three months and really wanted to get my travel money back. It was a little hassle to get the money back. But after several weeks of delay, I did. I just talked openly with the indigenous Shipibo shaman and we agreed on giving me a little of his salary every month to pay back. To make this happen, I also contacted the administration lady who came weekly to pay the staff, so once she came, I was in line to be paid as well.

One of the first things Francisco told me when I arrived was that his grandfather, also a shaman, had told him he now needed a woman in his life. So he figured he would like a woman like me to accompany him in life and support him on his mission to heal people. Someone

10 - Ayahuasca Trip 5

who would understand. Someone like me, he said. Oh no! Not another one of those problems. I had always felt being a good-looking female is a challenge without even wanting or doing anything. Looking good, whatever that means and in whatever varieties that occurs, may be a bliss for some girls. For others, like me, with my story and cloudy sense of identity (what I thought about myself), it can be just the opposite ...

That day, as we walked from my house to the center, Francisco said he would sing for me during ceremony at night to heal my childhood trauma. Interesting, I thought. What does he know? I was wondering what he referred to. Did he mean the suicide of my father or was he referring to the sexual abuse by our new tenant of the business a few months after that? Well, whatever. Everybody must have some kind of a worst childhood experience which becomes their trauma, I guess. I decided not to put out any ideas or paint pictures in his mind. I decided not to question what he knew exactly and just let myself be surprised...

It was really interesting and big what happened during that ceremony! Even though we drank pure Ayahuasca without any other herbal medicine mixed in, each batch was different. And depending on who of the two shamans was singing, what songs they were singing, to whom they were singing and with what intention they were singing, their singing had a different impact on us. The singing kicked off the whole Ayahuasca experience like blowing air into the fire. Things started moving. In the body, in the mind, in the perception, stuff was experienced more intensely, like taking off the anchor of a boat.

Both the shamans' songs and the intensity of my own breathing acted like an acceleration of the Ayahuasca journey. When they started singing the whole experience intensified drastically, as if someone had pushed a button. When my breathing changed, the intensity and speed of the experience changed as well. Deep breaths acted like paddle strokes.

Tonight, I don't have much visuals, even though I drank 3/4 cup. However, immediately emotions appear for the first time. Interesting, since I had not experienced any emotions during ceremony at all so far. Others did, I did not. I got messages about how life works, spirit, soul, duality on the material plane and so on. Now emotions came all at once!

As soon as Francisco moves over to me, which I didn't even notice, see, nor hear, I bounce up from lying flat on the mattress into a crossed-legged sitting position. As if an electric spark was hitting me. Ouch. Oh gosh! So much shame, shame, shame. Big-time shame. And guilt. Unbelievable, how yucky that emotion feels inside of me, and worse: how I feel about myself. I had no clue how deep rooted that stuff had been, stuck in lower layers, with me spending lots of energy to keep it down there, by distracting myself by keeping busy. Selling myself the idea that by doing something valued as "important," altruistic or otherwise would be recognized by my social environment, I would gain a kind of birthright to live, gain value, self-esteem, recognition. In reality, deep deep down, a totally different story was going on, without knowing why, and even without knowing that I felt really bad about myself. I was aware of some guilt program running in the background, a subtle fear of doing something wrong and risking to become guilty, risking to mess up the world, without even knowing why. A dead-end road. Nothing was safe when it came to "doing the right thing." I had this deep-rooted fear of doing something wrong and being responsible for other people's negative outcomes due to my doing. An old memory of the death of my father, which was clearly related to me doing something wrong, that's how life worked in my childish mind: You don't comply with expectations, you are punished.

***

Then there was the abuse of the new tenant of our house and business, a few months after my dad passed. In my mind, I "allowed" this to happen and therefore was guilty. I did not scream, I just didn't move, like paralyzed. Clearly guilty.

Now that Francisco sings for me, I feel like that little six-year-old miserable girl. I feel like that girl that has no more father, as if some entity, has ripped him from me and I was clearly involved in that situation, since it happened to me. Cause and effect. Clearly.

Even worse, I have allowed that man, Mr. K., who was like a role model for me to remember how a father could be, to touch me! How yucky is that. That night in the jungle I am that little girl. Endless shame, guilt and despair. Gosh! There is just not a slight bit of hope for me.

10 - Ayahuasca Trip 5

It is simply too late. I have lost my dignity forever. This is something that can't be undone. There is no escape from this incident. It is done. I have become guilty for allowing it. This is who I am. Ashamed forever for being who I am. And I can't fix it anymore, it is done. I feel like a piece of shit. Just much worse. In total despair. Absolutely no hope of deserving anything good in life, after this. I am crying my guts out. It just doesn't stop. Francisco keeps singing and singing in Shipibo language and I cry and cry. It lasts forever. Endless. Hopeless. Ashamed to be who I am. No way of fixing it. A broken piece of glass. Gosh, I had no clue that there was still that kind of energy trapped inside of me.

During twenty-seven years I have been forgetting the incident and controlling my emotions, then, I finally remembered what I had suppressed. I tried to fix the problem by facing my abuser. And now, still, I have these memories: how this man's hands and nails look, and how it feels to be touched there. How I feel with this conflict inside of me. I feel myself in the skin of that miserable girl who has just allowed some "father-type" man to touch me in the vagina. So there are still emotions to be healed.

As adults, we can only look at whatever we remember with the eyes of an adult. When I remembered the incident at twenty-seven, I interpreted what I remembered in a logical way. I could not relate to that girl that I was emotionally anymore, emotions were cut off, suppressed. At thirty-three years of age I certainly knew that it was not my fault being abused as a six-year-old. It was clearly that guy's responsibility to defraud my dignity. And I couldn't tell anybody, because the situation after the death of my father was even worse than before, very tense, dark, and critical, life threatening. I was always in fear that my mother could commit suicide. Even though I had been told that my father died due to a heart attack and I did not know that he actually had committed suicide, I still feared my mother could do so, just as if I had known the truth. I could not possibly tell her what had happened at that time. Too risky. I might have put her at risk to no longer be able to cope with the situation, young mother of three, just lost her husband, never really content anyway … And there was nobody else I could talk to. Maybe my cousin, he was ten years older than me and I felt as if he was my only trustworthy ally. But he wasn't there when it happened. He lived too far away from us. We hardly ever saw each other anyway. My cousin was the only person who seemed to see me. He took me the way I was. With him, I was not in fear of not being okay, being rejected for possibly, maybe even unknowingly not complying with expectations. He could see me. He cared. And I could feel it. He didn't do much, no special gifts or trips. But he was there, really being there. Present. Listening. Compassionate. Interested. Open. With him, I felt safe to just be.

But in this moment of abuse, I was freaking alone with my dilemma.

Then, at that time my mind immediately had already wiped out the memory of the abuse and I had to carry the weight by myself in my unconscious. In my mind, I had never been abused. Abuse was a totally strange thing that happened to kids, who then get very traumatized. I definitely was not one of them. I functioned well in society. Nothing had happened in mind …

Here I am, crying my lungs out. And Francisco sings and sings his soul out. It feels good. I feel blessed. Cared about. I feel honored. I feel worthy. Someone who cares! Truly cares without expecting a repayment in exchange.

I feel what I feel, ugly but true. And it feels good to allow myself to feel the truth without suppressing it. To let go. What a relief!

All my life I had been conditioned to pull myself together. Not show "negative" feelings! I hardly ever cried in front of my own mother when I was deeply sad, after my father's death. I hid in my room and when someone came, I pulled myself together perfectly. Nobody ever saw me. I hid. So I stayed alone.

All of a sudden, my body starts moving all by itself and the spine lengthens: I roll it up from this deeply bent down, shameful posture vertebra by vertebra. I roll myself up into a perfectly aligned lotus posture. Head straight, heart open, shoulders wide. Space. I finally occupy my space. I allow myself to occupy my own space. There is a "me" inhabiting that body. I have my dignity back. My worth. My birthright. My life.

It feels like behind me in the celebration hall someone is sitting on a throne, a throne with a lotus-shaped wooden backrest. Some elegant strong lady is sitting behind me on that wooden throne. So I turn around to see what is going on. And what I find is that it is me! I am that lady now occupying that throne! My throne. Weird and beautiful. Then I see a man who looks like a meditating Buddha right in front of me. He sees me for who I am. Nonjudgmental and respectful. There is light around him. He must be some spiritual guy with no hair. I see energy moving up into the skies in spirals and pastel colors. I feel strong. Then rage comes in. Hohoho. Rage. That's totally new. Wow, how powerful. In my belly, I see a big fat smile, a mean smile from a man with a big mouth and big teeth and space between the teeth, a very tanned face with wrinkles. He has a really mean look. He looks like a Mexican from an old western movie. Is this a part of me, too? Do I too have this potential inside of me to do anything, even evil? Then I see the bold guy again and myself opposite him, both being drawn up into the skies in spiral movements, smiling. Beautiful and blissful.

* * *

I got my integrity and dignity back that night. Thanks to Francisco and a whole load of circumstances that led me there. I am grateful.

Another long night followed after that dramatic experience. I hear footsteps in the jungle. It freaks me out. I notice fear and real big physical tension especially in the shoulders and neck, all tight. I decide to call upon the Mexican-looking monster in my belly and be strong rather than fearful. I can bring the monster out now, I am no longer a little girl. I can defend myself. I know what is right and what is wrong. I am not a victim.

The footsteps were just leaves falling from a big tree, hitting other leafs, I realized later. But they sure sounded loud, close and scary ...

Then I hear a whistle. It sounds like the shamans are making this sound to induce more spiritual energy. At least the effect of the whistle that I hear is the same as the shamans blowing aguafuerte over us. I am okay now. No more fear. It's okay. Whatever or whoever this is, it is there to help me. If anybody is there in person or in spirit doesn't matter. It's okay, I am protected. I feel it.

Another very long exhausting night. Right after the little fruit dish that Gomeru, the kitchen helper, brought at 7:30 I went back to nap. It

Headless Chicken

had been a breakthrough experience, and I was very exhausted. Very old sand on the bottom of my vessel had been shaken, mixed up and cleansed.

That's how I always saw myself: like a grain of sand, a tiny part of the beach, that which makes the beach a beach, together with all the other grains. So that the sea, the skies and everything else can be together with me, the grain.

11 - Two Days Off

Excursion to Iquitos

Surprisingly, I am asked to go to Iquitos. Surprisingly, because I had worked my mind around the idea of staying away from civilization and distraction for longer, like a precaution to not freak out or so. In this brand-new situation, I found myself having days without any real duty or at least not that I would know about in advance. A whole lot of time to question. What do you do when you have nothing to do? What if you can't do nothing all the time? Funny odd mind.

The managers were going to the city for two days in order to receive new clients, do some business and Internet stuff. They invited me to come along, so I could practice Spanish with them while we were in town. Cool! And very good for them. A rather entertaining environment would keep their minds in a state where they would not be focusing so much on the fact that they don't know how to speak Spanish, but learn by doing, playfully.

In the morning after breakfast we took the retreat boat and left for Tamshiyacu, following the river into the Amazon. There, we refueled and picked up some locals to give them a ride into Iquitos. The whole trip takes about an hour and a half. A very meditative boat ride. Especially the first part to Tamshiyacu, taking shortcuts passing tiny rivers and wild vegetation through the Amazon jungle. Adventurous. Heading into the Amazon at that one super-wide spot we saw dolphins! Pink dolphins! I didn't know that they existed in pink. I didn't even know that dolphins can live in rivers. And since I came to the retreat so spontaneously, I didn't do any research on what to see and explore either. The boat trip is special. Really timeless, because you are so involved in being there with all the impressions that you can hardly think. At least at the beginning when everything is new. The magic of traveling: being present, not thinking, not thinking ahead, nor thinking about the past. The dolphins seemed to just enjoy themselves all day long. Playful. Harmonious moves. Fun. Easiness. Serenity. Masters of their being.

We hung out a little near the dolphins at the river joint and turned off the motor. One of those moments when you don't know if this is heaven or earth. Just amazing. Endless. Timeless. Going nowhere. One.

As we continue, nobody speaks a word. Maybe the other people have thoughts in their minds. I don't. Maybe the left over, from last night's ceremony. I feel connected. One with all. No thought. No need to think. That would spoil the experience. It just is, without me interfering. Glorious.

Arriving in Iquitos way down at the riverbank we climb up the hundred or more old, uneven, tiny and partly broken wooden stairs to street level. Iquitos is mostly flat. The three of us take a moto-car and drive to the hostel to check in. Jeremy stays at the hostel to do some Internet work. He takes care of marketing their place and answers questions of potential visitors. Allison, his wife and also manager of the retreat center, who had problems to open up for unconventional alpha state language learning, and I take off. As soon as we leave, I feel a different vibe. Both Allison and I are having fun. We both enjoy the wild movement in town. It is not pretty, according to our Western standards. In fact, houses are mostly worn out, shops have funny-looking cheap stuff when it comes to clothes and shoes, very basic products in any sector. But we did not find it ugly. For us the whole experience was rather exciting and exotic. Authentic. We spoke Spanish all the time, and the girl who had broken down in tears a few days earlier for not understanding everything we spoke, was having a heck of a time. And so did I. We talked half body language. I let her become more independent, by not helping her so much and she went herself to get what she wanted. We practiced basic stuff such as asking for what you want. I would only help with a word of vocabulary or two and have her experiment her new skills. She stopped thinking about what she knew and when or whether she had learned that before. She did not think whether it was correct, what she wanted to say. Instead, she was absorbed in the process of living and experiencing the now, in a flow type of state.

11 - Two Days Off

This is exactly what I had intended with my alternative teaching methods before, but her resistance was bigger than her curiosity to just check it out and give it a try. Now, here in Iquitos, she could no longer resist. The present moment caught up with her.

I know this mental mechanism myself. Instead of just going ahead and experimenting, I would not even get started, finding a huge amount of reasons why I might not be able to do this. Considering the amount of energy and creativity that went into this process of finding excuses, why not to do something, the potential got stuck somewhere without ever being allowed to appear on the surface. This mental mechanism of resisting, finding excuses, judging, finding reasons for why not, etc., not only appears in creative processes such as painting a picture or writing a poem. It can also be at work for anything we have not done before. Anything that is strange to our habits, our habitual thinking, feeling, acting. Just imagine or remember how many times you have heard yourself or others say, I can't do that, I am not good at that. Or, I have never done this. This is not my thing. Nobody of our family was ever good at that. My teacher told me I didn't have the talent for that. Our family is not good at mathematics. Et cetera, et cetera.

Now, in Iquitos, Allison could break through the mental barrier that had kept her from allowing her to experiment. We had such a good time. I also realized my own barriers ...

Enjoying the day just for the sake of enjoying the day. No need for higher purpose, making sense, being productive. No need for distracting the mind with alcohol, drugs or loud music. We could just be and enjoy, just what the message during ceremony meant: go play, enjoy. You are here to play and enjoy! No need to go anywhere further with it. You evolve anyway, just by being present and living fully.

It felt good to break the ice after the difficult start. Alison realized that I was rather a friend than an opponent who might be criticizing her. She must have been criticized a lot and was very hard on herself. A level of perfection was not only to be reached, but excelled. Get better! What sounds like a great virtue can be a drag. Never good enough. Always in search of something else. Something more. Never content with the current state. Always something missing or something could or should be better, according to that little judgmental bitch in the brain. How exhausting! How well do I know this.

Headless Chicken

Having lost my father at a young age, I also got into this habit. Unconsciously. I was absolutely convinced and truly believed there was something wrong with me. I desperately had to improve myself in order not to be a potential threat for anybody, due to my ignorance of not knowing what was wrong with me. That was my deep-down fear. A mechanism without being aware of the unconscious shit going on in the background. It took me until my mid-thirties, when I was faced with very advanced skin cancer, that I found out that nothing was wrong with me other than some ideas about myself. When I was faced with the fact that I might die soon and had to be re-operated immediately, "next week might be too late," something clicked in my mind and I knew I had to change my attitude toward myself and toward life. Instead of changing what I was or who I was, my very essence, I just had to change the way I was thinking about myself, my programming, and my unconscious beliefs. The part that made me feel bad about myself was not how I acted, felt or talked, but an unhealthy mindset. My very essence was absolutely fine, actually beautifully lovable.

But before that time, I had not realized that my mindset and my essence were not the same. I was always trapped into thinking. And that thinking made me feel a certain way. All mind, but not mindful. A victim of habitual thinking in circles and programs. Then, I would unconsciously use so much creativity to justify my emotions and interpreting the world the way I felt. In other words, I would find explanations for feeling bad about myself by picking out only negative stuff of what I saw in the world. Projection. Or, interpret the situation negatively. In fact, it was as if I constantly looked for excuses in the world that would justify my habitual feeling bad about myself state. How sick is that. Well, not that sick, contemplating about it. That's exactly how any training works: you learn a rule and use what you have according to the rule. Mathematics, social behavior, what you have been told as a kid. I was told: shame on you. With no bad intentions. That was probably what my mother heard from her mother. Some kind of a way of disciplining and teaching.

Now that day in Iquitos, my student became my reminder and my lesson, showing a pattern that I had lived unconsciously before as well. The idea, I am not good enough, got stuck in my mind naturally. I remember as a kid I would see in the world proof for not being good enough. I would interpret situations in a way that would prove

11 - Two Days Off

my belief. And I would totally ignore situations that would not fit my beliefs, situations, where I could have been proud of myself. I conditioned myself not to reward myself hardly ever.

I was not aware that I had interpreted the world around me in my unique way to make it fit to my beliefs. I also did not know that I did not know the whole truth. It all started when my father died.

Age six I remember waking up one day in my small bed in the morning, panicking. I had not been aware of anything different that day; however, instead of going down to get dressed and have breakfast, I ran away to the tenants upstairs and told them something bad had happened and that I was afraid. That day, at 6 o'clock in the morning, my father had walked through the kitchen, passing his wife and his mother to go to his workshop. There, he took a rope and committed suicide. And I felt something without knowing. The rest of my family wanted to protect me from the cruel truth and decided to tell me a white lie. I was the only one, the youngest of three, who had been told a different story: to me they said he had a stroke. He worked too hard. Too much worries about the money.

I will never forget the funeral. I was sitting with my favorite cousin, farther back from the rest of my family, who had sat in the first row of the church. We were sitting in the middle of the crowd, away from the priest. That day I thought I would probably die as well. I could hardly breathe from crying. It was okay. I would go with my dad, wherever he was. It didn't happen. He had left me behind and God took him. If there is a God, he doesn't like me …

It is amazing how secrecies can create deep-rooted problems due to withheld information—or lies. The fact that everybody else had a different version of what had happened messed up the idea of how I saw myself: That year I started school. I didn't know anybody. I was a tall and pretty girl. I became self-aware during that time and started to think about how I appeared to others. And how others behaved toward me, or what I observed in others through my own tinted perception, would hard-wire what I thought about myself.

What I saw was that people would talk with their hands in front of their mouths so I could not hear. That irritated me. I interpreted they did not like me. I assumed there might be something wrong with me.

Headless Chicken

I reckoned, they know what's wrong with me, even though I had no clue. And I would see some kind of slightly odd behavior toward me all over the place. I felt they were different toward me than toward others. That's how I started believing and being totally convinced that there was something fundamentally wrong with me. I felt separated, wrong, excluded. What I did not know, was the fact that they knew the truth and I didn't. And again, they wanted to protect me, and not hurt me by telling the truth and speaking openly about my father's suicide. Age twenty-one, I accidentally found out about the truth. When I finished high school I had taken off to go far away to learn another language. I knew I had to leave and clear out the stuff that I felt infected with. I had witnessed a lot of dark times, sadness and negativity. I knew I had to wander, to find out what life was about. So I had left for the Canary Islands to learn Spanish. After two years I came back and found my mother sad, sitting in the kitchen. I asked her what was wrong. Nothing, she pretended. Yet, I dug further. Finally, she would open up to speak. My father, referring to my stepfather, had been so bad to her again, she explained. So I asked what he had done. She said he had told her, if she continued behaving like that, she would end up like in her first marriage … "That's ridiculous," I said. "Why would he get a stroke?" "You still don't know?" she asked. What would I still not know? Then, she told me the truth, that he had committed suicide and they only withheld the truth from me to protect me. That was it. All spoken. Fifteen years of twisted reality gone in one sentence.

Nobody had ever talked about my father anymore in all those years in order not to stir up the old stuff, not to dig into the sadness or make anybody sad. They simply had forgotten that I had been excluded from the truth.

I then understood why people had been looking at me the way they looked at me in the village. What I had interpreted as their rejection and separation was in reality empathy or pity. "That poor girl." And since I was the only one in the whole village who did not know the real story, there was some kind of truth behind my idea of being excluded. Now I got it. I could see clearly how I would interpret what I saw in the world the way it would fit to my beliefs. It was so obvious. That's why later on, I could relate easily with client's beliefs and take them seriously, instead of trying to change their thinking by manipulating them somehow. I understood the way their minds worked and how that made them feel. With compassion.

11 - Two Days Off

A part of the thinking mind seems to act like a doorman called ego that wants to make sure nothing new comes in that could harm the current system's beliefs. What we perceive as reality can be just a protection of what is currently stored on the hard drive! If we know it or not, if we are aware of it or not. It works that way, like a mental movie projected on the screen we call reality!

So there in Iquitos, I remembered clearly how kids can easily be programmed in a way they don't choose. They don't choose that program and often nobody really chooses. It is an ugly consequence of unawareness. Hardly anybody wants to do harm purposely. And yet, a lot of harm is done.

And this is how so many people end up in self-sabotage, being hard on themselves, never feeling good enough. A simple error. A misunderstanding. A lack of communication.

That day in Iquitos, I could just go around, flow, enjoy and so did Allison. We both gave ourselves a break from habitual unconscious thinking and feeling, the deep-down critic had been exposed as a lie and we could just be and enjoy.

Time passed fast in Iquitos. I almost bought a bunch of local handmade instruments I had fallen in love with. Something to play with. Decided just stick to my habit of downscaling possessions and travel back at least as light as I came. Not much shopping, but lots of fun. The next day we went back. I did get a couple of light, cheap, comfy cotton dresses that I ended up wearing day by day for the next year. Great investment!

12 - Cutting Down Resistance

Less Hard on Myself

January 7, 2014

Ayahuasca trip 6. It's strong today, the medicine, Shaman José says. So I take only half a cup. It takes a long time to start until I can feel it. As if it doesn't work at all today. The mind is busy thinking, not allowing a break to let the energy flow between body and soul. The freaking controller doesn't want to get out of the way. I take it easy though. I know putting stress on myself makes it even harder to break through. So I just observe my impatience. Then, I remember that magic word that I had learned at hypnotherapy classes: Egal. Egal in German means *it doesn't matter*, or, nothing really matters, it's the same. Then, suddenly the mind relaxes a little, opening up to the space to be explored. Yes!

I remember the British tao teacher who taught me to put the mind in the back of the head, drop the weight, and open the heart. That didn't work for my brain, not at the time when I first heard it. Nor now. Too confusing. The focus and energy stays in the thinking process, like an obsessive-compulsive disorder. I don't take it like a disorder, but rather as the typical Westerner's inability to shut up that freaking mind. Then in the ceremony hall, during a small gap of nonthinking, the door opens so quickly that I forget about worrying whether the medicine works today or not …

I see the big stuff, which is made of the same moving energy as the small stuff. The small stuff is a structure of moving energy that makes the big stuff. And in the small stuff is still

12 - Cutting Down Resistance

smaller stuff and still smaller stuff and it is all the same: moving energy, vibrating. I see the endless universe in each particle of an atom, or an electron, or a proton or whatever we call the tiniest of the tiny. Nothing ends. It is all connected. One. Something I could never have seen with my regular mindset. I would have just not allowed this possibility, since it did not fit into my current state of conscious knowing and understanding. Later on, I hear or perceive a voice. This voice is not inside of me, it is bigger than me. A voice saying: ... and then it (the manifested stuff in the world) all dissolves into the big void of nothingness and there is nothing left, only light.

At that moment, that very moment, the shaman lights the candle. The ceremony is over. Purge a bit. No big deal. Getting used to the cleansing process.

Then all is peaceful, and for the first time there is energy in the body to walk straight down the beautiful wooden staircase into the rain forest night.

On the way out I meet Dave and Randy, the hairy, sweet New York boys. Lovely people. Like almost all of them. Very individual. Like all of them. Totally different, even though a similar look: Long hair, long beards. It all feels like one family: the German Peruvian, Daniel, Joey, Doris, Alexis, Roman, Tyler, Colin, Jeremy, Allison, Rocio, José, Francisco, Lucy, Gumaro, Juan Antonio, Walter and the other workers and the animals and the plants and the rain and the wind and the sounds. Maybe a consequence of the drug Ayahuasca, or just the habit of attracting amazing people or the other habit of seeing beauty in everything, even a shit-hole.

Colin reminds me so much of Philip, my stepson, and Christopher, my son. My stepson had passed away four years earlier during a vacation in Israel with his dad, my former husband, and his siblings. It was my son, age sixteen at the time, who found him lying dead in bed next to him. Philip would be thirty-three now. Colin was only twenty-five or so. I see Christopher in him as well, just a bit older, as tall, slender, compassionate and handsome. Just a good guy. Colin was only twenty-five and had already been in the military for four years

Headless Chicken

as a paramedic. Iran and Afghanistan. Two wars. Lots of scars.

As far as I understand now, for spirit to manifest on earth, it needs a body. This life on earth is like a theater stage where spirit can create, heal, evolve, expand and get entertained. "Good" and "bad" are two sides of a scale, the same thing, two extremes. We choose by the way we see, think, focus, talk, create.

Why wars? Killing spirit? Killing soul? No, only some egos manipulating others to kill bodies. Nothing seems to matter to them. The problem seems to be the disconnection of many minds and bodies to their souls, or maybe I should say unrealized souls, individuals that don't realize that they are not what they think they are: their roles and labels, the profession, the family role, the reputation, the amount of accumulated economic wealth and especially their egotistical idea of what is right or wrong.

We are some kind of unrealized potential. An energy field of endless possibilities that has lost the connection to the source, God, the Almighty. Who am I? What am I? Am I what I think? What I feel? What I look? All that changes all the time. So what makes me, *me*?

So many people out there suffer from not feeling connected to their hearts. I am one of them at times. Living in the head, far away from here and now. All thinking. Back, pondering over something past or forward, fantasizing scenarios. If you reduce yourself to a chunk of flesh, with a sophisticated computer in the head, it is difficult to find meaning. This lack of awareness or the illusion of seeing what we call reality with these local eyes, feeling disconnected from heart and essence can make one go nuts, if you dare to question and look closer. Going around in circles, pondering, searching, questioning. But the answers are not in the thinking mind, they are in the "big" mind. I guess what I perceive as big mind, some call "the (quantum) field" or God. These people, suffering from disconnection, can be easily manipulated by others, by other seemingly spiritless bodies, those who have also lost connection to their innermost essence. Those whose highest interest may be accumulating

12 - Cutting Down Resistance

personal benefits of some sorts. That may include some church, "important" speakers, anybody really. People manipulating weak, disconnected or fearful people.

People with such a mindset then really assume that this is it, my body, my life. Get the most out of this for me, myself and I. Like a dis-ease, a lost soul connection, and a lack of a deep connection to other human souls. Incarnated spirits make their journey into the body and now their minds don't understand who or what they are and what they are here for. Without feeling compassion and unity the purpose of this life experience becomes quite dull and meaningless.

To heal the world from shit, we must start from within and feel, sense, intuit, not just limit our being to thinking. There we can feel a deep sensation of connectedness, peace. Warm, velvety, cozy, limitless peace. Then we live in a creative state of flow, not through controlling and thinking. I have come to the conclusion that there is a high possibility that around 90% of thinking or more is meaningless and simply stupid. Repetitions of old or other people's thoughts, like playing the old disc over and over, from generation to generation.

I saw myself in an endless pond, as a kind of lotus flower opening up! Felt loved by a male, but no sex, just pure love, felt every cell in my body and mind and soul loved. Even the wrinkles, small bumps and aging skin. Fearlessly loved. Amazing. This is real. Really start loving every cell of myself. Finally. Nonjudgmental. Just acknowledging what is, without judging, without labels and boxes.

Be hungry. Have cravings! Cravings to do stuff. Travel, work, meet people, contribute, exchange, be a part of every puzzle I encounter. Do my best and be free, non-attachment. Feel the urge to be creative. Dance, paint, perform, play, learn, travel. Could take one of those boats on the Amazon for a few weeks over to Brazil. Even though I am curious, it doesn't feel quite right now. I came for a work exchange. I could do some jobs, make money, just make enough money to travel and live good on the way, spend and give back to the people, stay in flow. Start liking to spend. No, the flow never ends. Nothing ever ends, at least when it comes to energy. I always had more than I needed. Definitely. Thank you! Whoever You are. I even know that I don't have to work. I am helpful anyway, that's my nature, that's what I am. Even though my thinking mind can't accept the idea of not having to work at all, reality has shown me that really I don't need to work! The more I dare to trust, the more joyful the process becomes. I started getting jobs that I love and was paid well for them as well. It didn't feel like hard work for sure. More like mission, something you enjoy doing, from the heart. All it takes is the awareness that it is my choice and trust.

This is the first night that I am able to write after a ceremony without having physical restrictions. It is midnight and I am in control of my body and also have energy to sit and write. Before, I was content when I was able to direct my body into bed. That healing from Francisco sure worked. Got my body back and can now play. Anything. Know deep inside that I need to use my voice and body in the future to express myself and share. Details of the development of my vocation will show up as I go along.

January 8, 2014

Again, in the morning I go back to bed, to stay in "the space" after Gumero brings fruit.

Experiment: put my mind in the back of my head and open my heart. Immediately, frequency changes into a vast joy, expansion, abundance, connectedness, playful vibration that wants me, my presence, my essence in the body to creatively join in and play. Weird and beautiful. Remember a conversation with my friend Angela from Germany. She has been successful in her PR career. After talking about what we had been doing since the last time we met, with a focus on profession where we were, and where we were going to, etc., she came to the conclusion: I think you just want to play! She referred to her perception of my work situation. Yes, was my honest answer. Work and career are not so important to me. But meeting, sharing, exchanging is. I like to be helpful and inspiring. I believe in joy being more important than security. What some

12 - Cutting Down Resistance

call hard work, I call excitement for your vocation. "Sharpening the saw" is a metaphor by Stephen Covey referring to the saw as your instrument, your talents, abilities, knowledge, capacities. For me "sharpening the saw" means continuously being present, training body and mind, expanding my capacities or awareness. For me the daily rituals to sharpen the saw and stay tuned were more important than figuring out a way to accumulate wealth and security. To me, downsizing and simplifying meant freedom. Luxury had a taste of dependency. I like sleek minimalistic luxury. Less is more. Security is an illusion. I have made good money. Had a reputation. Built a house on the Indian River on Hutchinson Island. Flew a four-seater Cessna. Nothing is really that important to me anymore. I want to be free. And yes, I want to play, enjoy, share joy. I believe in good vibrations. Negative vibrations will show up as dis-ease, bad mood, discontentment. Goes without saying. Every moment is my choice, if I am aware of it. What I make out of this very moment and I don't refer to a mental power exercise of talking golden shit. It is about acknowledging the shit in the gold and the gold in the shit and make a decision at the very next crossing, what part you choose to focus on and go for it.

That morning I do a shamanic journey to the lower world. I had learned this way of journeying in Lake Tahoe from a couple who lived a half year in Hawaii and half year in Tahoe. Once a month a group of locals and this old couple would gather at a community center and go for a shamanic journey. Two or three people would play Indian drums. The monotone drumming got you in a trance quickly. My power animal was a ram named Kalim. Again weird, but I saw it without usage of any drugs. I had seen dozens of animals during this session, but when I saw the ram, I instantly knew that it was my power animal. And the name popped up: Kalim. Generations of native Indians had done these ceremonies during hundreds of years, so, why not? After surviving cancer, I no longer needed scientific proof of how things work which I can't see with the naked eye and that had not been acknowledged by a Western university. It was good enough for me to know that they worked. Like music.

Headless Chicken

Kalim, my power animal, says: you are a playfully healing artist. Your presence, vibration and creativity is the tool to heal. Spreading positive vibrations. Your job is to play with the vibration. Use the big mind, tap in, and create healing vibrations. Forget about other work to make money. This is your job this time. This needs to be done. You need to do that. No more doubt. People need people like you. Money flows to you with ease. Go spend it. Bringing it back into the flow, exchange, share. Care for your individual vibration in every moment! This is how you attract what you need in abundance. You are powerful.

I had left the journey to write this down. It feels like "it" is writing for me, through me. Is "it" my higher Self? Or even God? Some angel or spiritual being? Does it matter, anyway?

Conclusion: No drugs needed to tap into the space beyond the thinking mind. The message I get is very much aligned with what I explored during Ayahuasca ceremonies. Whether my local mind makes this all up or some bigger entity designs it to fit doesn't really matter to me. What matters is what impact the message has on my ability to live a "rich," happy, inspiring life. Rich to me means abundant, valuable, not limited to monetary value.

Then I have an encounter with a super sweet baby bee. This happens after the shamanic journey, in every day's regular perception, what we call "real." The bee sits on the left top corner of my book as I write. She seems to lick the paper for minutes and sticks her long nose on the notebook while curling her tail rhythmically. I call her Bruna, the name of the second child of some very dear friends from Argentina, I asked her to come back some day. I remember visiting a shaman lady ten years ago in Mallorca. I had never considered consulting a shaman, first because I wasn't aware of their roles and abilities, secondly, because I wouldn't have known why I should see a shaman in the first place. I went with my dentist, what I thought of as a real down-to-earth person. Very successful in business. I had never done weird stuff like that. She invited me to join her and I came along to find out what it was about. The shaman read: your soul was broken into 100,000 pieces through trauma. It looked like a beautiful very delicate golden shimmering, shiny clear crystal ball, inside the same stuff as outside: nothing, pure potential, Energy in empty space. Golden shimmer ... .

Hmm. That's how she perceived the real me? Then, she continues: People of bees come with their queen to stay with you, gluing the 100,000 all back together with golden pollen.

And since that time I am always happy when I see a bee. It protects me.

That was sweet. I started liking weird stuff. Later on, studying hypnotherapy I found out there is some scientific proof for using stories for healing purposes, tales or stories as the great Hypnotherapist Milton Erickson used to make up to inspire people to heal themselves.

As soon as I got into the regular busy mind mode, or what we erroneously call "real world," I started wondering. The so well-known "yes, but"-ego mind questioning: yes, but what am I supposed to play? Yes, kind of a nice idea, but how do you make this come true? What am I supposed to do exactly? A song comes up in my mind. I sing. I never sing songs I have never heard before! Since I had never heard that song before, I recorded it, to remember.

It feels like today I start the rest of my life in flow. At least in that moment it felt like that ... . I am powerful, beautiful, creative, expansive, never-ending vibration. My presence walks and vibrates and receives and sends all the time. I am part of the puzzle. I am part of the big mind. The universe. God. Remember my presence, my being, consistency, magic, life, an abundant adventure. Joy fills up my heart. Heartfelt vibration. No words for that really.

Feel that some special guy will be coming into my life soon. Easy! Me, all open, vulnerable, brave, loving, real, honest, beautiful, ready, fearless. Pure life, grateful to be in the body and create. For the first time. Wow!

13 - Ayahuasca Trip 7

Spooky Experiences to Clear Out Goals

January 9, 2014

So far, I had never really felt fear during ceremonies. Whenever the idea of fear came up, I looked at it and saw this is not worth it to invest any fear. There is no threat. No good reason nor excuse to be fearful. No reason to run away or fight.

It has been two weeks since I came here. It's my seventh time exploring the spirit world and that part of myself that I had not been consciously familiar with. So far it has been exciting. And healing. Mind blowing. Confirming. Releasing. Considering that I didn't even plan to do the plant medicine at all, I really kicked it fearlessly, as if nothing could harm me. Some people go nuts doing this stuff.

This time, it's a totally strange and different experience. Got a treatment from Francisco again when he came one more time to help me fix stomach and chest pain. I have had huge pain in the kidney area and in the neck. Hmm, maybe there is still fear. Years ago when I first moved to Majorca, I had this pain before. Kidney sand, they said. I just went on with the pain without thinking too much about it, as if I knew once the origin of the problem is addressed, the symptom would go. Francisco is a real healer. Again, he said he was looking for a woman like me and for some reason I have no problem to tell him exactly what I felt: I was not looking for a man like him, I meant physically, for a change. He was small, strong and wiry. Before I never cared whether the guy was physically attractive to me or not. All I cared about was his soul, the essence that

13 - Ayahuasca Trip 7

drove him. As if men came without a body. Unfortunately, I totally overlooked all physical and mental problems such as extended ego or drug problems.

Some major change has happened. Before, I would have gone round and round to try to say something I did not dare to address directly, so I would not hurt the other person.

Now, I could be clear and direct without fearing to do any harm. Francisco is the man like Iggy the Irish Flamenco miniature Viking king type guy I hung out with for two years to realize what he wanted is not what I want. And also to realize, he had made me 10,000 bucks lighter, my savings were gone. Francisco was physically like Iggy, just native Peruvian. Small, skinny, defined, marked hands, strong features, intense hair.

He said he can help me energetically to sort out my neck, transcend ego and support me in renting out my flat in Mallorca to make a little money. That's what I had asked for. And everything happened. Well, except that the ego is not all gone. Also I told him I was singing this morning. Turns out he had turned on his phone to speaker and played a song by another shaman from Pucallpa, sent to him this very morning. I listened to the song on the phone. It was exactly the song I had hummed. Shamanic. Weird. Very weird. By now, I wasn't totally thrilled anymore. OK with what is, even though my thinking mind can't explain. Probably some kind of synchronized humming over the ether type thing.

Francisco said he wanted to teach me. I should record his singing during ceremony, so I did that very evening. When José was singing I was completely knocked out. I had zero memory of anything. Just an experience of deep sleep. Nothing. When I woke up Francisco started singing and I recorded him. The recording job seemed to keep me from traveling. Interesting. I have no visions or emotions, just observe what is happening in the room as if I wasn't journeying at all. Even though it seemed like I had not been traveling to the other world and my experience of what I had witnessed that night seemed to be in a regular state of mind, it was in some sense deeper or

Headless Chicken

had different subtle layers.

I could feel Joey, who had pain in his right shoulder, was being healed. And I took on his pain! All of a sudden I feel a mega pain on my right shoulder. At first, I thought I could have done something wrong and hurt my shoulder. Then I realize, it's Joey's pain! Then, I am pissed off about myself. I always had this empathy problem. I could not only feel what people feel. But then I would take it on, as if it was mine. That was not fun.

Then I relax and remember that I am like water. Anything can run right through me. Also his emotional mess or pain. Dave is flying high making sounds like he was experiencing tantric sex or something. Then somebody else says in an annoyed tone of voice: "Can you please keep it down!"

I catch that wave. I feel it right through me. Don't know why but the young kid who just arrived seems to be having trouble too. Then I get this message: your ego mind is judging the situation. However, this is not real. In reality you are Love vibration, just vibration, moving energy. This magnificently manifested world, thoughts and feelings are just projections, nothing is yours, they are just copies on your hard drive, so you have a software to play the video game. Don't take it serious! Your own true thoughts are thoughts of pure creativity, some thought that nobody else ever thought before. Everything else just is! Been copied and repeated ...

Conclusion: if ego names it good or bad, it doesn't matter. It is not real, anyway. Egal doesn't matter. It is what it is and that's it. Nothing to think about, just leave it for now. Next question: what about right and wrong? Good and bad is also a judgment and changes according to the social environment you are in. In some cultures it is okay to eat your neighbor to survive. What does matter is to make choices that you sense are positive for "it." And "it" is you who decide. Do not just think and let some old program decide for you!

Feeding negative emotions by unconsciously focusing on fear, doubt, anger, jealousy, etc., is what it is, looking for what

13 - Ayahuasca Trip 7

could be wrong: it creates a negative projection and you see exactly that projection: the nasty part of the world. You can create whatever you decide. Consciously or unconsciously. Everything is possible. If you are not aware of how this process of life works, you risk to run some old program and create your world accordingly. So as a manifested soul in the material world it is indispensable to make decisions according to your essence, what you feel and sense; this is the way to go, right here, right now. You feel it in your guts and in your heart. Focusing mentally on the good and bad can take you off track because you are subject to being conditioned by other people's thoughts, ideas and programs. Morals that have nothing to do with you. Remember Hitler! Or religious power games and manipulation and the crusades. We can't continue to just blindly take something on.

What if with this kind of awareness you just float, flow through conflict, challenges, let go of old negative emotions and be a manifestation of your true essence, not just a puppet that is directed by others? Sounds like heaven on earth. So at the end of the day, good and bad are mostly learned, conditioned judgments of your cultural environment. What feels good on a subtle level beyond thinking, that is the real path. Maybe love is a good attempt to give a name to this state of being. Scary, adventurous, surprising. Can't fail.

Just trust the process!

Ayahuasca at work. Challenging. Not fun. Well, sometimes yes, despite the puking. Not horror for me, just getting rid of shit, cleansing, vomiting, diarrhea, emotional discharge and stirring up the bottom of your mind. The process takes all night for me, long after midnight when the ceremony ends. Feels like wild thinking. Feels like shaking it all up, to bring it into a new peaceful form. It's nothing new, really. I do remember the baby blanket my friend Susan from Florida gave me as a gift for my first newborn. Follow your dreams, it said. I'm not 100% sure, yet I have a feeling that you can create your own world, which is not real anyway, by choosing your thoughts. Seems to work for me. When doing so, it is important to focus on a deeper level, not the thinking brain level, but heart level, sensing rather than programmed rethinking. That's the trick and that's the challenge for the thinking mind that wants to be right and know it all. Everything is perfect. Or at least has the potential to be perfect. The evolution happening is enlightenment. Once we know that we know without knowing with the local mind, we have the key to open any door. Knowing without knowing from somebody else. Deep knowing even though you can't possibly know, because nobody told you … . "People" start learning their true nature, becoming aware of themselves being spiritual, becoming aware of their freedom, power, choices, fun, creativity, joy, love, oneness with all there is, enlightened. They stop suffering.

My job this time is to inspire visions, hope, that every being is part of the one big miracle and can set himself or herself free to create whatever miracles they want.

In detail, specifically: inspire to focus on the miracles we want to create, inspire to discover the spark, life energy, inspire to experiment, expand, find joy, your soul's joy, what sets you free, what you came here for, what you want to focus on.

For me it is creativity, the state of flow, no thinking, letting the energy run through this body and mind and live from that awareness. Concretely: playing with my vibration, the intention, the key, to inspire, be at my best, flow, joy, heart. Love the body and the power of the mind, appreciate myself and the manifestation of "it." Share. Contribute, be the One, together with all there is.

More down-to-earth: sing, paint, dance, travel, coach, exchange, learn, expand, play, act, model, use body and mind as tool of the soul, heal with use of intention, tuning in, compassion, love, being a tool of the One, an instrument of God. Not a slave to the ego.

The more I learn "to stop thinking," be the rider of the horse (the horse being the thinking/monkey mind, "me," the rider being the essence), the more I get into that desired state of flow, the more I can feel what is truly important for me to thrive in this lifetime.

13 - Ayahuasca Trip 7

Shall start with meditation again!

Ayahuasca and Francisco are cleaning the shit out of me. My belly and intestines are like a volcano and I kind of like that burning fire! No fear, but life. Energy. A lot.

January 11, 2015

Ayahuasca trip 8. This day I woke up knowing that I would take a full cup at the ceremony later that night. No pondering. More like a picture showing up on my screen. So I do so at night. Take a full cup. Got that message. Go for it!

Very intense! Went into the ceremony with a positive joyful feeling which just expanded. Before, I had been super alert and cautious, as if the mind just did not want to let go of control. And nauseous as well. I do have complete faith in the process. Same message again: shift from operating in the brain to operating from your guts, stomach, manipura chakra. Okay. Again!

This is your compass. Get this message over and over again. Intuition. Let go of compulsive thinking! Tap into real sensing with focus on real, which means here and now, that what really is. Feel compassion and love for Doris, the depressed girl, who had been getting on everybody's nerves. Cannot remember much. Could hardly return after ceremony and hung out there probably another couple of hours after the ceremony ended. It was like I was drunk. The body was, the mind not. Messages over messages ...

Go for the joy!
Choose your experiences!
Focus on what feels good!
Stay with positive people!
Protect yourself!

Pamper yourself first from now on. You are an expression of all there is. You do good to all by pampering yourself first and loving yourself, caring, healing, thriving. This is your job. Spread the good vibrations. Help people awake from the mundane dream to their true nature. Inspire.

I ask: what do I really want? That question had always been complicated for me, because I was doubting whether that was the true heart desire or just some fancy idea that I had picked up somewhere. But I do know. Travel, Machu Picchu, yoga, surf, develop and perform some kind of show, create vision, light, faith. Yes and also money to do all that. Money is an energy. Let it snow! Ha ha. Act in inspiring movies. Play that exact character that suits your mission, your being. No bullshitting. Learn another language or learn to communicate with natives somehow. Sign language. Heart language. Play an instrument or create music. Sing. Attract a real, caring, loving, twin soul life partner. Give speeches and seminars.

Note: I am writing this book two years after visiting the jungle. Reading the notes as I am writing it all down still feels wild, after having lived in an environment that seems to ignore all that nonmaterial truth … And it is all lining up as I saw it …

January 13, 2015

Ayahuasca trip 9. Again I take a whole cup. No visuals at all. When the chatter in the minds stopped true words came out. Saw my dad. Hermoso! A handsome, loving, caring, compassionate father. Tears. Deep sadness. A sadness that I had not allowed myself to experience ever. I miss you. When my father died, I learned to wear a mask very quickly. I suppose right after the funeral. I committed to play my role in the family and agreed with what everybody did: not ask questions! I only cried secretly. And not too loud, so nobody could hear me. I controlled myself, to shut off half of me. The energy to suppress all those feelings was tremendous. I guess I felt strong. At that time since age six I had not realized that I could use that energy for myself instead of against.

Message. This time I hear:

13 - Ayahuasca Trip 7

What you are looking for is inside of you!
Trust your gut feelings.

Your dad is around watching over you.

People dream of you. Get out and share, let beauty shine, spread your light, be timeless, ageless. Be. Just be.

We are all brothers and sisters.

Fulfill your wildest dreams! Now!!!

Your wish is my desire! (referring to my individual wish being the desire of the big one magical energy that drives the universe, God) Wow! My wish is God's desire??

Love, affection, cariño.

Harvest love, enjoy love, one love, you are part of it. Included. Feel it! Appreciate it! Celebrate it! Empower it! Spread it! Be a role model. Love yourself intentionally! Put out the intention to love yourself and all there is and enjoy every moment! Celebrate life!

Now, I notice that I was disconnected from my own love by the thinking in the mind, precisely, the ego. All it takes is intention. Then I feel it. I feel it, I feel love in the heart, warm, comforting, trusting, safe, sound, solid and yet fluid, endless, timeless, true, indestructible, real.

Francisco comes and sprays Agua de Rosas on me and puts my head straight on. (I don't remember exactly what I mean by that. I can't remember him touching my head. I think it was an energetic adjustment, like clearing the throat chakra or something.)

I see my father again, Reinhard. He is a good-looking chap. See a dark, black, beautiful man with the same deep look in his eyes. This is my match to walk along with. I would recognize immediately. Had a clear question: Ayahuasca, please tell me exactly what you want me to do next! I get the whole picture and I now want to know what exactly I am supposed to do work wise! How shall I spend my days in order to contribute, create, share and exchange? All I get is: play, perform! Movies (uff, ha ha), shine, be at your best, be a role model, use body and voice, travel and work, travel for work. Dance, speak, act, give talks, create a show, live your wildest dreams, be who you want to be. It is all a matter of power, choice and intention! Go play! Play is your work! Have fun and receive the fruits of your actions!

Boy, that sounds wild. Sure doesn't sound like a proper job description. Can I really just go and play?

January 14, 2015

Ayahuasca 10

Decide to take only half a cup. I just feel that's enough and I trust. It's still strong. I vomit. No visuals. Lots of yawning, which is emotional discharge. I feel the change in the brain, physically. Need to touch the back of my brains a lot. Rub it. Feels like I was restructuring the inside of my brain. No thoughts. I like it. Gave out a wish to "Mother Ayahuasca," as everybody else calls that which I call higher part of ourselves, that which we can access by taking Ayahuasca or by going into a very deep meditation: I would like to rent out my flat while I am here. I say so and let go. Feels like I'm growing out of the child-space into the female-sex-space. Enjoy your femininity. Play! How? Experiment! Wait for desire, don't use thinking mind!

Noticed yesterday that I actually had been afraid of men without consciously knowing so. I now own my power. Be the person you want to be in the world.

Don't fight, be like water! That's your technique. Take every opportunity to learn. From every incident you witness and participate so you can learn more. There are messages just for you when witnessing situations. Your projections, the way you look at yourself, you can become more aware in every moment

13 - Ayahuasca Trip 7

and learn. Take it as a free gift to change anything you want to change.

The chap next to me looks shocked just when I yawn with the mouth wide open, without putting a hand in front. Interesting. Maybe because of my lion's mouth wide open. Who knows what he just experienced. Whether it is my interpretation or his judgment, I kind of appreciate the situation. It is what it is, pretty unimportant. I can see clearly now. I can distinguish between mental interpretation of a situation and what really is, without any judgment. It is up to me, whether, I put myself in a fear mode or in a love mode. It all depends on my freedom to choose how I respond. Therein lies the piece I had been searching for. That's why peace starts within. Only by us cutting vicious circles of projecting negativity can we transcend and transform.

14 - Done Healing

A State of Feeling Terrific

January 16, 2015

Something inside of me feels whole and complete. Maybe I am done healing. I do feel terrific. Even though I haven't been practicing any yoga, just a bit of tai chi, no brain fuck, no questioning, just being and listening. Love it. Think of Brazil. Imagine going to Brazil. And other South American countries. Shall go when I feel the time is right. I know that I will know exactly what to do when the time is right. Will stop trying to figure out making decisions on the topics that are not due yet. Remember my kids and my friends. Have no plans, no cravings of missing them, just feel love sensation thinking of them.

Francisco had more dreams about me. He saw me coming to him, being his partner. Shit, I think. No drama, please. Then I remember, it is my freedom to respond, so I respond calmly and clearly. There is no problem. I can feel it. I can feel exactly what is going on inside. So I know, no matter what other people dream, all I have to do is just be myself. He comes in the morning before breakfast telling me about his dream at night (a night without Ayahuasca ceremony), he saw me as his life partner who also works with him. I tell him quietly my vision of using art, being an instrument of communication to inspire and open up people. I tell him, maybe I am his communicator in some way, intimate partner without being a sexual or life partner. I can talk very clearly and direct with ease. Just to make sure he understands. Funny enough I had a funky feeling when he first hugged me putting his arm around my waist ... he is so much shorter or I am so much taller,

14 - Done Healing

that he embracing me just reaches my waistline. I had that very clear funky feeling that moment and my mind kicked in trying to convince myself that this feeling was probably just my messed-up interpretation of the situation due to childhood stuff. A messed-up mind kind of thing. And it wasn't. I can trust my sensations. I did feel a slight fear in that moment. Not that he would do anything I would not want, but fear of male-female conflict and I would not be able to say no or stop. Now things are clear. Yes, there is a conflict of wishes and dreams. No, there is no problem because I can now just be myself, fearlessly. We just have various wishes and dreams.

January 17, 2015

Went to Iquitos just for an hour online. Today, I feel sad, missing friends. And it's okay to want to see the kids and some of my friends, Val especially, Annett, Audrey … Am emotional and that's it. I just observed. As long as emotions don't take over life in such a way that they would limit the experience of now creating a ping-pong game between thought and emotion and ultimately some state of suffering, as long as I can just feel, observe and be okay with the feeling, I am free. That very morning before leaving I had a very hard time to say goodbye to Kelly and Dennis, formerly from Seattle, who now go back to New York. I have a soft spot in my heart. We had talked about love. Noticed that I had closed my heart to protect myself and therefore could maybe only give some love, but not allow to receive, like a radio station that sends and doesn't receive, which is, in a way, not being able to listen and not being able to allow to feel. Only able to project. Sad!

This whole trauma stuff most of us seem to go through is not that bad after all because it forces us to remember who we are. And this is nothing we do by thinking, but by feeling with the heart. I could empathize and feel and feed others. I was totally closed up toward myself inside. Like a bunch of love trapped in an invisible realm, separating the others from me and me from myself. This is changing now.

Headless Chicken

Also, I am hungry now. I enjoy eating, finally. That's giving Love to the body in form of delicious food. Since I was a Pescaterian anyway, I truly enjoyed the simple food we ate in the jungle. I added on some local superfoods that I got in the market in Iquitos. I had been losing weight and could not eat enough, so I mixed extra maca powder, kamu kamu and aguaje to everything I ate. And that was basically rice with some veggies, sometimes with fish or eggs. The fact that I was hungry was a good sign. In my teens I had a skiing accident that resulted in a broken jaw. After months on liquids, I started liking that freedom to no longer have to eat what was on the table. In my family, the rule was: Mother fills your plate and you don't get up until the plate is empty. Slowly slowly, I started my silent revolution and stopped eating. I tried to pretend I already had eaten. Although I had never been big, or concerned about my weight, I entered the long-lasting serious eating disorder. Only later I realized the reason for that. I did not look for attention. I simply did not like living.

Nobody ever asked me why I would not eat. At the time my answer would have been: I don't accept to be forced any longer. I need to be free ...

Told Jeremy to focus on Spanish and coaching training more intensively for the next few weeks, because I might travel sometime.

He had asked to me to give him coaching training as well besides Spanish classes. He realized that I could establish fairly quickly some kind of confidence with every new client, and he couldn't. Most of the visitors addressed themselves to me when they needed support. Not only because I was the interpreter, for those who didn't speak Spanish and wanted to talk to the shamans, but because they felt I could understand them. I did not judge them. They only found out I was a life coach later or not at all. So that part of empathy and understanding that Jeremy wanted to learn from me had been my treasure and my drag.

So far, I don't know when to travel, where to travel to and how to travel. Or whether to travel at all. Just feel this tickling

14 - Done Healing

excitement.

Having hardly any Internet access is a really good thing in this case. That's what I want to learn so badly, to let go of constantly thinking. I want to trust and learn to allow to be guided by some force that is bigger than myself, and act through my heart. Surfing the Internet with the monkey mind is rather hindering that process. When the time is right things will appear even if I will not know in advance what to do and where. (Turns out that I get some unexpected visit later on and end up traveling to sacred valley.)

I did imagine my friends would be coming. Some of them knew where I was and desperately wanted to come as well since they have been thinking to do work with shamans and plant medicine since a long time. I figured, time will show and whatever happens, happens. Best is to put the ego aside and free the path.

I am always at the right place at the right time. I can trust to do the right thing as long as I really listen inside. Focus on love, heart, warmth, compassion, joy, happiness, peace, light, beauty and harmony. Act from there. Not motivated by fear.

The trouble between Jeremy and Isabel, new managers of the resort, is none of my business. That lady's daughter, daughter of deceased Scott Peterson, had inherited the resort in the Amazon and the mother, ex-wife of Scott, the founder, now tried to manage the place for her daughter. Her former husband had recently died in his early sixties. He was a well-known Ayahuasca specialist and many people loved him and appreciated him for his work. There were also a lot of negative stories going around here and in the Internet about him. Alcohol and sex abuse. After knowing how misleading our minds can be and how judgments can harm, I decided to just leave those stories as they are, without getting involved personally. I did not even know that person. Why would I need to judge him?

Isabel, his ex-wife, had contracted the young Australian couple to manage the resort business. They had some kind of 50-50

Headless Chicken

deal after expenses. She used to appear spontaneously, out of the blue without announcement.

They had a lot of discussions about management decisions, expenses and who had the final say. In this conflict Jeremy had hoped I could not only interpret but also mediate between the two parties. He had not told me that little extra job before and soon after arriving here I found myself in the midst of the personal crisis of the couple and the professional conflict with the owner. So I acted as a witness and mediator. Both parties were not really interested in the other party's view, arguments, needs and wishes. They were both pretty much closed up, with a set idea about the other party. Also, the discrepancy between saying one thing and doing another was not leading to any resolution. The situation already was very tense and it felt like they both wanted to escalate the conflict even more forcefully to get their way. Two egos fighting.

The rainy months almost gave a poetic touch to the whole story. Intense and dramatic. I decided to stay on my love vibration and stop caring about other people's vibes. Not really stop caring, more stop getting impacted. I needed to care for my vibration first of all. Only then could I mediate, witness, serve as a non-biased observer.

For some reason I had found more clarity. Finally. All this exploring and experiencing this space beyond what drove or controlled me before had a positive result. Now, I was no longer trapped. I could perceive without limiting myself, without fearing to possibly harm anybody or suffering myself. Free.

15 - Ayahuasca Trip 11

More to Explore?

Ayahuasca had opened a door to deeper levels of my being, so I could heal.

It did not feel like a very pleasant ride, rather exhausting and challenging in every way. There was an amazingly beautiful experience followed by a terribly painful one. Painful for both body and mind. Something tells me not to stop quite yet. There is more to explore. I just don't want to make the error to get trapped in comfort, when I have a chance to expand more. It is not a calling. More of a "make sure." More thinking than feeling. So stop or continue? What's the risk? Just keep going and see ...

Since quite some time, I go to ceremony by myself at night and also back home by myself. I no longer need the guide. Sometimes, when I get ready to leave for ceremony and gather things together in the evening, the pillow, the blanket, the water, the toilet paper, the bug spray ... at latest when putting on my rubber boots and grabbing the torch, that sensation of feeling terribly sick already starts. The human mind really is a tricky toy.

Again, this time I only take half a cup. Both shamans also confirmed that this was the optimal amount of "medicine" for me at that time. Calm mind. Finally! No more wondering when the journeying would start, when is the medicine going to start showing effects. No more doubting whether this is working for me at all or whether it doesn't, like the depressed girl, who says it doesn't work for her at all. Some kind of letting go is happening. Instantly. Wow. No spectacular visions nor messages in this ceremony. And each ceremony takes about five hours at least. For some, like me, the journey continues all night.

Headless Chicken

Only this time, to trust that a calm mind can tune in all the time. No need for tripping forever.

I relax. It has been quite exhausting to go all that way, doing intense journeying for weeks. I know I don't want to become an Ayahuasca shaman or so. I only did this because it was an invitation to explore deeper. At a cost! I was physically worn out. Some people lose it! I took the risk and felt safe along the path, despite the unknown stories. And I wouldn't want to miss the lessons. Or rather the confirmations. Deep down I knew what I experienced. But with the monkey mind keeping me busy, I could not listen, nor trust.

They say that physical strain is like physical "work," that feeling sick, in pain and drained is a signal that the medicine was working. I don't know. I just know how ugly it feels and if you don't judge it, it's not that horrible, after all. Like giving birth to a baby. The pain is soon over and you are left with the gift.

The physical pain helps definitely to make one surrender obsessive thinking. The discomfort is stronger than the monkey in the mind that keeps on bringing up thoughts over thoughts and wants all our attention all the time.

So now I know it is time to bring this kind of awareness that I can access during ceremony into every day's awareness. Hmmm. Sounds like I now would need to become enlightened or something … Why should that be so scary or difficult anyway? All it means is bringing light into the darkness. For me personally it also means to transcend ego, this idea about who we are, the labels, stories, conditionings, programs. And yes, it has a scary touch to it. Fear feeds Ego. You don't want to be excluded from the tribe for being different? Or just scared, what you see in the dark within yourself?

January 23, 2015

Ayahuasca trip 12

Didn't plan to do so, but took very little Ayahuasca that night and had a lovely ceremony. Love!

15 - Ayahuasca Trip 11

What is love? I ask. It's what people do! It's how they act in general and toward each other. Again I feel Ayahuasca is not an external entity, but as I would say, it helps me to open up to that higher or deeper part of myself, that which is connected with "all there is," God, all entities of the universe. That path, door, pathway that can access any information by consciously tapping into the field, the one energy and potential. The me, the it, the pathway, all one. In that sense Mother Ayahuasca is a highly intelligent plant that opens me up to that loving part of myself which is part of you, which is everything.

Today this ceremony tells me: accept the beautiful woman that you are. You are not the kid. You are a woman. Love is free. Love is a gift. Love is a donation to give and receive.

Giving and demanding in exchange is expecting payment in exchange. This is not really true love. The intention behind the action does matter. Having good intentions and not acting upon them doesn't help either. Is it about giving a gift for the other or is it to get something out of the action for yourself in the first place? That's OK too, just be aware of your wheeling and dealing. Be honest. Practice love! You receive what you give, because there is only one big pot. You are the pot. When you give with expectations you want to control the law of love. That doesn't work. You exclude yourself from the big pot as if you were the only cook. In reality everybody cooks. That's why some say we are all Gods.

Nine months earlier I had just filed for divorce. Second marriage. After "giving it a try" and moving to the States to make this trial period possible, we had to marry in order to be able to live together. So we did. No big deal.

After the first winter I knew and also felt this is not right. I blamed it on myself. Thought I should sort out myself. And my former husband willingly provided me with books and special alternative therapists. I just did not trust myself, my heart, my guts. I still thought there was something wrong with me. How crazy is that?

I gave it three years, even though I knew and felt after the first winter that this was not for me. I learned a lot in the high mountains of

Headless Chicken

Lake Tahoe. Especially when I stayed home alone with the dog. My former husband went to LA regularly, for work, family and friends and haircuts. He preferred to fly by himself, since money was limited and I did not make a dime during quite some time. Sometimes we drove together by car, so I would get to see something else. I also had friends in LA that I could relate to, a connection and friendship, not just chatting. I had missed that human connection in the gorgeous environment of the high mountains. Our neighbors would meet up for happy hours. Fun too, just a bit boring after some time. I didn't really connect with others like that.

In those years in the mountains, I only made friends with very few selected people. Those became friends. We met like once a month and really shared. Since my husband had back problems, he preferred to take a plane to LA instead of driving for eight hours or so. Most of the times I would drive him one and a half hours to Reno, to the airport, so he could get the plane instead of driving eight hours in the car. This whole experience got me to meet my own ego tremendously. The monkey mind calculating how much time I would sit in the freaking car to drop him off, drive home, then pick him up and again drive the same way home. I was driving myself nuts, telling myself how stupid I was spending six hours driving to save some time and money. I did it "for him" without heart, hating myself for not just saying "No, I don't want to do that." And, without talking much about it either. Just like any small issue, you don't agree with. The ego starts revolting making life hell, just because of a conflict, of what we accept without really accepting. The solution could have been to say: No. Or, okay, I drive this time, even though I don't feel like it and think it is stupid in the first place.

The times alone up in the mountains were very revealing and interesting. I like my own company. I started finding an outlet for my creativity and recorded audios with tools I invented, that I sent to specific clients who had contacted me sometime before to ask for advice. So during this time alone I used to walk in the woods, have tons of creative ideas and recorded audios creating metaphors and images to help people expand their minds.

I loved that experience because it was most astonishing for myself to see how creativity just shows up out of nothing. Despite the fact that my judgmental mind would chatter and judge my efforts to be useless

15 - Ayahuasca Trip 11

because nobody would ever find those hints on YouTube. It was about the very moment. Just for me enjoying myself creating. Interestingly, years later, I started using that material much more for clients.

I witnessed and learned about his ego and realized I had to have this experience in order to realize, accept and transform my own ego. It is so much easier to accept someone else's shortcomings than your own. At least for me.

For some reason, I hoped my transformation would somehow have an impact on my surroundings. And yes, secretly, I hoped something in him would change in such a way that we could really open up and meet. Meet beyond the egos. Trying to express myself, I only gave it one effort each time and gave up quickly when I was not heard. It cost me too much energy. Instead of just focusing on what was good for me, daring to be honest, showing up as who I was, I tried to manipulate the situation, I did not leave it to the big wise field. He was very giving and in a subtle way expecting. Even though he might not have been quite aware of his expectations. And I was busy trying to fulfill expectations, without daring to really show up as who I was. I did not want to show up too much, whatever that meant. Until one day I broke down in tears and said, "Our relationship is all about you." And he responded that this was correct. Of course it was. In hindsight, we had a great time, many times and learned a lot. In hindsight, I believe you feel when you meet the right one. And not only you feel it, the other one does too. This was not our case. We appreciated the other one for many reasons, but we did not feel that this was the one. And still we gave it a try ... I wasn't ready. He probably wasn't ready either. And it still was a very valuable lesson in life. Nothing is for nothing.

I seemed to have a problem with receiving love because I was holding back that part of myself. The shadow part. It was easier to place myself in the skin of the other and take him first. That's a nice idea, but I exclude myself. How can you be a partner in a relationship when you don't show up as yourself? You may be loving and caring but you are not truthful to yourself or to others. This ceremony is about learning to open the heart and fearlessly receive love, no matter how vulnerable it makes me.

Headless Chicken

January 25, 2015

Wow. Felt another attack of self-doubt, questioning, feeling insecure, nervous. After all this work with Ayahuasca. What a drag! So, Ayahuasca doesn't really cure it, but cleans shit out and shows it. You still have to do the work. Looks like this is a lifelong job. Is Ayahuasca making me dependent?

The challenge is not some trauma stuff itself, it is ego trying to stay in control. Freaking part of the mind.

No sleep, insecurity. What bullshit! This ego, trying to edge God out, trying to be God, fearful of losing control to something bigger. I don't need this anymore! I don't want this anymore. For me, God means the source, all there is, the magic behind hearts beating and evolution happening. I am super-tired of that ego stuff. Connect with the source and be home, safe, happy, content, joyful, who you really are. Nothing more to it.

As soon as the analytical, local, thinking mind is quiet, I am. I have no problem with a situation as long as I don't think. "Yes, but blah blah blah ... " Yes, problems don't solve themselves without us saying what we want. We need to give some kind of a hint to what we want. But that doesn't happen by thinking. It happens by feeling. Feeling and sharing. Thinking comes afterward if necessary. Find possibilities and choose. Sometimes, it is about being patient, that's a real challenge.

Grateful for the lesson. It is true: when it becomes very uncomfortable, the chance is good to really learn important stuff. Getting stuck in complaining doesn't boost the lesson, but prevent the learning. It is like a merry-go-round and round and round. You need to get the lesson, stop complaining about ego or circumstances, accept it as it is in order to take the decision: I am going to get out of this going around. Once out, we see clearer and feel in charge again.

Ayahuasca 13

I just keep going to ceremony. Like a habit. Another habit ... Very strange experience. Took very little. This time I hardly tripped. Saw some beautifully dancing plants, I am part of it, of this endless creativity. Besides those few glimpses I was fucked up all the time. The belly sounded like a roaring ocean, mosquitoes in my ears, as if they flew directly in there or were on speakers, eyes itching, ants in the pants, not literally, but that was the sensation I had during this ceremony.

I had strong diarrhea for quite sometime, over a week or so, from eating Ceviche, local raw fish soup at a stand in Iquitos Harbor. Yes, one would think, do not eat raw fish, but I was hungry at lunch time and that was all there was before going back to the jungle. And I knew there was no dinner at ceremony nights. They can eat it, I can eat it. Not taking into consideration that the locals have a different type of bacteria going on in their systems.

The shamans gave me natural medicine from the trees that stopped the diarrhea. The workers went every day to get me a cup of white, slightly sweet and thick, sticky milk from certain trees by cutting slightly into the tree. It probably took half an hour or longer to get a smaller cup out of the tree. I felt appreciated and honored for so much caring. Even though the diarrhea stopped, I was still sick inside. The body still struggled with bacteria. I had stomach cramps, felt sick, went to the toilet many times a day pooping yellow whitish. But I had total trust and faith that with time the natural treatment would help. At no point did I consider getting in the boat to Iquitos to go to the hospital. It took a few weeks, and I was weak, but I got over it. Just like the locals, waiting till it is gone. That stuff they gave me is what they give to the kids. What I had not considered was the fact that my immune system and body had a totally different state than the body of jungle kids. And the death rate, due to diarrhea was much higher in the jungle than where I came from.

The visuals that night are brief and amazing. Yes, we are all one with everything. But these physical experiences in the body are most uncomfortable. Painful. That's the last one, no more ceremonies, that's enough. Done with discomfort and pain. As soon as the candle is lit and ceremony is over, I am as energetic as can be! How bizarre is that? During ceremony I had been constantly moving the body. Just couldn't find any comfort in the body. And afterward, I stretched and contracted muscles intensely and felt super fit for the first time. It just happened.

And then I heard something say to me, without me asking: stage, performance, body and voice. Gosh, again. After the ceremony was over. My own voice? Ego? Imagination? I didn't want to know that kind of stuff. Too scary. Stage work? Hilarious! And yes, I did want to hear that. I was just super scared of the possibilities way beyond my comfort zone. All that range of possibilities had been so much off my radar, out of reach, in some way unacceptable, considering where I came from. Therefore I have been fearful to face that side of myself. Fear of failure. Fear of being excluded. Too weird. Egal doesn't matter, I was telling myself my magical mantra. And it worked. What happens was, as soon as I said those words, I stopped thinking and judging. Peace. Anything is okay. It just is.

Doris shared her experience: she has been fighting against negative energies all the time and had to focus constantly in order not to be pushed into a big black hole. Depression, again. Interesting. I was just the opposite. I didn't fight. I just went on with it to see what happens next. I saw the negative, dark stuff and the beautiful light stuff. Maybe this state of surrender is the key. And no judgment.

I also had a very uncomfortable experience. Felt like I was hardly tripping, except that major insight information, seeing that we are all one. Seeing it visually and feeling it. Then, the attention switched back to that discomfort being in the body.

Then after the ceremony I experienced these creativity attacks: see myself on stage, doing a show, talking, laughing, crying, sharing. Kind of cool and yet very freaky for the local mind. When I hear the new guys talking, Jack from Canada and Jean

15 - Ayahuasca Trip 11

Luc from France, I notice that I am like on fire when I share something important to me. I can feel energy moving through my whole body to express. Head moving, face, arms, hands, upper body moves. Feels like I really have to do something with that energy. Express. Share. I had asked so many times what my next step would be. Show me what I have got to do next. That's when the stage appeared. Best thing is not to judge and allow this way-beyond-comfort-zone possibility. Maybe the one-woman show will come up next …

A few years earlier I had met this lady at a conference in San Francisco. We just saw, greeted, hugged and started to talk as if we knew each other for years. She was a shiny, voluminous, black woman in her fifties. A coach. We exchanged business cards and a few weeks later she called me to tell me that she saw me on a stage doing a one-woman show. At that time, my ego was blocking the entrance to something totally new and different. But in the meantime, I had been signing up for improv classes in Spain. I didn't think about show or stage at the time. I only wanted to explore this space beyond the thinking mind. I didn't worry so much about the language, it was in Spanish. Since improv is all about not knowing what comes next and then acting in the very moment what feels right, I hoped it wouldn't matter too much if I didn't understand everything the other performers would say. It is what it is. Coming back from Peru I actually started being on stage doing improv in Spanish. Something I could never have dreamt about. Nor imagined.

I share my experience with Doris. You are fucking ridiculous, she says. I noticed that I seriously like what she says. Don't feel offended, no need to say anything. I'm just fine, no matter what anybody judges. Really wish for this state to stay. I am okay with you having an opinion. None of my business.

January 26, 2015

Do a shamanic journey in my hammock to visit the higher world. I ask that being in the higher world that I call Cleopatra, because she is so beautiful: what is the topic of my stage acting?

Headless Chicken

Love, she says. From the head to the heart. Meditate on love. Feeling the love. Be love. Then, all you need is to open your eyes in every day's life and you will find your way following love, signals, synchronicity.

Love!

January 27, 2015

This is a great gift that I am getting here. My whole belief system and habitual response is being changed. I wonder if the dormant parts of my brain are being ignited slowly slowly as well. I try to keep a calm mind and not to think too much about anything, so I wouldn't get into analyzing. Analyzing uses only maybe 10% of the brain, that information that I am already aware of. All of that I already know and have been using in the past. I need to grow beyond that. That's the whole idea. Expand, create, explore, evolve. I want to ignite more! At least expand. Thinking is not useful for that.

As I write this now, I just saw the film *Lucy* with Scarlett Johansson and Morgan Freeman. Actually, I watched it just yesterday: they talk about exactly that, accessing full brain capacity ...

This last ceremony was so subtle and so profound. Very busy mind, unquiet. Very hard on the body. Heat. Unpleasant. With visions in the plant world or spirit world, dancing in the air or ether and water and vacuumless space. And I was part of it— there was no me only THE or it (Spirit World looking like a plant world, dancing). Brief, pleasant experience. Then, when finally the candle was lit to signal the end of the ceremony I felt super powerful energy streaming through my body, like electricity, high voltage power, energy, light. I became bubbly, talkative. Go home and dance? Didn't feel like that was the right channel to direct this energy into.

Felt like I am empowered, now I have got to take it into the world. Not just dance by myself alone, but share that pulsating force of all there is, spread the message, be creative,

15 - Ayahuasca Trip 11

entertaining, whatever. Grrr. About to explode.

The following night I decided to stay home. Not in for Ayahuasca but practice yoga and meditation. Good sleep, I wake up early, study Kundalini tantra. Wonder if what I experienced is something similar to sushumna awakening or so. Definitely moving energy in the chakras. Egal. It's doesn't matter!

Had a major physical pain, again like childbirth and felt brain restructuring at the brainstem and in the back of the brain, in the front and in the very center of the line that connects the ears. There is this central point of the brain which I felt like a tiny drop that contains a miniature version of the universe. And all that without ceremony! No Ayahuasca needed. Yet, will do one more full power Ayahuasca.

Thursday, January 1, 2015

Getting really bored. Wish I could walk or do something. There is hardly any place to walk to, since the rainy season has flooded walkways throughout the jungle. After all those days of the runs, Lucy the cook prepared a special tea for me. Three times half a liter, I have to drink every day for five days. It's amazing. Despite being worn out physically, I started becoming very energetic and want to act, do something! Like a cleaning, clearing out the pipes and now, full energy can run through.

Wants, wishes, thoughts, lots of energy, enthusiasm. Think of pantomime, dancing, acting classes, 5Rhythms, getting a job in the bakery or just anything, going to Berlin working on fairs, exploring the model and acting markets over there. Something. Also think of surfing in the north of Peru in Mancor. Would love to visit Brazil, and and and. The mind keeps chatting away as it always does. I don't fight it. Just observe without giving too much attention and importance to it.

Next Monday I will go to Iquitos if nothing changes …

Headless Chicken

Ayahuasca trip 14:

Take 3/4 cup. Not strong.
Uneasy, impatient, fed up. Interesting!

Just observe emotions and thinking, this is the human plane in the body. We can think, therefore we judge and duality exists. Do not attach! So I don't, just observe the movie. No visuals, except one powerful picture:

See myself and Fatima's hand entering the top of the middle of my head into my brain, like placing or installing the chip from the soul in the mind. Fatima's hand is a symbol of Arabic and Berber countries, supposed to ward off the evil eye, I look up later.

Very interesting, didn't even know the meaning of Fatima's hand at that point. Message: you don't act with your local conditioned educated 10% mind, but directly through your hands. You are already on the path that is prewritten. Get out of your way! Stop pondering, wondering, doubting, comparing, thinking social stigma stuff—instead, listen inside and be guided. You are protected.

January 31, 2015

During several ceremonies now I got the message to stop Ayahuasca and start meditating regularly, so I do. The information, the knowledge and wisdom I need is already inside. It always was. All I need to do is turn inward and listen. I am all prepared. I always was. Just didn't have the patience and the trust.

Today I feel a sense of deep peace without a reason. Starting to recognize any situation as a learning opportunity—good and bad. Feel free from attachment, free to choose, free from fate, but full of faith and power of thought, mental power. A few days ago Jeremy had told me, my "husband" had contacted him! He referred to my second former husband, I had just divorced. He wanted to come. Sounded like drama. I did not

15 - Ayahuasca Trip 11

think about it any further. Free. No need for emotional roller coaster or fear of being judged. No, the fact that he wants to come doesn't bug me anymore, since I know I am free in every moment. I can discriminate, make meaningful choices and respond wisely to any situation.

Jeremy and Allison came back from Iquitos. They still have had a lot of hidden bullshit going on. I could feel it. They want me to stay another six weeks. I want to stay only four weeks, max. Allison has childhood abuse memories coming up and is in chaos. Jeremy is being attacked by clients, Isabel, etc. I listen. And meditate.

In the evening Jeremy visits me at my house at 7 PM. It's dark. Just got back from my walk to the treehouse. He desperately wants me to stay another six weeks. I want to stay only four and then travel. We shall see. We'll leave it open for now.

He still hasn't refunded the 50% of my ticket as he was committed to pay, nor show up for classes, nor put any time or energy into his Spanish studies. Tell him that. No big deal, just facts and possible consequences. All good.

Wake up at five. Meditate. Again, asked to listen. Hear: Focus and create! Use time for project creation. Shame shame shame song comes up. Interesting. Do a one-woman show on shame? I start singing out loud. Fun! Then I fall back into sleep and dream. Then I get up and write morning pages, my diary of whatever appears, like hypnotic writing without thinking. A separate little experiment I had started doing. The first thing in the morning when getting up, taking a pencil and writing without thinking. Just like I did on the plane to Peru, where I got these insights and messages. In that state we seem to know it all, without Ayahuasca. Amazing!

Do yoga! Meditate! Write concept! Ask for help! Get inspiration from people around you!

Headless Chicken

February 7, 2015

Ayahuasca 15

Still go back to the ceremony for a special mission: Pascal, Freddy and I want to do a joint experiment. We all go in with the same intention and then share. Pascal is the guy from the Cirque du Soleil. Jeremy had told me I should definitely meet him and hang out. We would resonate well. And in fact, we connected instantly. Honesty, depth, sensitivity. Since he arrived we listen to Jiddu Krishnamurti talks after dinner until late night, on the nights off Ayahuasca ceremonies. It felt a bit like siblings, both similar age, he gay, which makes it easy for people from opposite sex with sex abuse childhood traumas to open up.

Freddy was a young kid from Norway, a little older than my son. A brave, honest, natural guy in his twenties with a story. The story I didn't know at that point. I just had a feeling. He wanted to teach me jujitsu, God knows why. So you could find us on the dining room floor wrestling. Maybe bizarre for box-thinkers. For us it was pure fun. The three of us had something in common. And we connected. So I did it once more. We went to ceremony for our joint experiment.

We asked the same questions to see what each of us would find out: How can we be in the "big mind space," the plane beyond words, senses and illusions in every moment?

How can we get over ego?

That was the purpose of our ceremony. We all asked the same question. We all got different answers. Individual answers. Answers that fitted our current state of awareness.

My answers were: Be yourself! Be your essence without the story! Open your crown chakra! Be yourself, not your story!

How do I open my crown chakra?

15 - Ayahuasca Trip 11

All it takes is having a truly felt intention! Put it out! Trust and let go! Forget about it! Allow it to happen!

By now I had learned to be okay with any answer, even though my thinking mind would not understand. My mantra: Egal, it doesn't matter! That's what kept the habitual thinking patterns hanging loose, so I wouldn't end up in endless circles of questioning and doubting. I just let it be, even though it did not make sense for my 10% hard drive. So I let go and forgot about my original intention. After a couple of hours or so I get the most painful and scary experience I had so far: I can feel mega electricity in the body, all over, up to the top of the head. There it felt like a burning bright crown, like an energetic connection, open to whatever is up there. Burning, like a head in flames from burning hair or so. Had I not had painful experiences before, like giving birth and biting my hand, I would have definitely freaked out that night. Freaked out from pain.

There I am, experimenting, and here I have the direct answer, very direct: feeling like Bart Simpson, except, his yellow crown is my fire-hot burning crown. A tube has been opening up. A wide tube all open, through my crown, diameter of approximately twelve or fifteen centimeters. Scary shit. Really weird. And yet, I knew exactly what it meant. I had asked for it and I got the answer. I got the feeling. This I knew was like a one-time experience. That won't happen all of the time just for me to remember to open my crown chakra. It is open. All it takes is to remember. To be aware. To set the intention. Just focus on your open crown chakra and you can be free of ego. Not trapped, but the master of the ego is bigger than the program. You can see it instead of allowing it to use you.

Also: be forgiving. You see your own and others' ego problems very clearly. Do not judge with your tamed ego! Be forgiving. Do not impose your knowledge or your opinion, unless asked for. Instead, be there for them. Be kind. Be loving.

Also stand up for yourself! Being able to be yourself now and not your story comes with responsibility. You know now that soul urge and true heart desires come first. You come to earth with a mission and that's your first priority. Otherwise, you abuse your being and don't function well in the body nor in the material world. Be "self-ish" first. That requires listening to your senses, feelings and intuition. You know exactly what is a true heart desire and what not. You know exactly when you project your own stuff onto others, when somebody hits your trigger, and when you truly feel something here and now. Those are the feelings that guide you. Do not suppress, reinterpret or try to change those feelings. They are here to guide you. If you do so, you misread the message. The purpose of those feelings is to give you directions. If you manipulate them in some way, you blur the direction and there is no clear vision of where to go.

Also: ask questions! Sit in silence, be patient, receive the answers. Tap in regularly! No need for Kundalini yoga, etc., you got it all and it is activated. It doesn't go backward nor can it be undone. Now be responsible and clear in every moment, open the crown chakra, be forgiving, compassionate, and yet selfish, be yourself and stand up for yourself. This life comes with individuality. Without separate body, no interaction, no playground, no growth.

Also body is like a shell, a vessel, a vehicle. However, it comes with senses and feelings to report back to the source. Do not twist or fight. Accept what is. Otherwise you mess up the communication to the source and your essence is receiving the wrong messages. Then you're stuck. Instead, allow, observe, have an intention without being tied to the how, to the outcome! Detach, let go, let it happen!

Sunday, February 8, 2015

Interpret at ceremony for Shaman José without taking Ayahuasca myself. Rocio, who usually translates if needed, had gone and they needed someone to be there to translate for the guests who didn't speak Spanish, just in case anything was happening and they needed assistance. Interesting experience. Five new people; yoga people, photographer, lawyer couple from Chile, and the girl that seems a bit disturbed. I have

15 - Ayahuasca Trip 11

been moving over to Doris's house since the retreat was fully booked. Pissed off since all of my stuff got wet. It rained inside. In fact, I got pissed off even earlier. I really didn't feel like getting into that negative vibe with my sensitivity and empathy. Maybe now is the time to get over other people's shit. Allow them to learn and go through their stuff without getting involved. You can still be compassionate. But you don't need to get sucked in! That's why I had to move to Doris's, so I could learn. It felt like I started kind of liking being pissed off. It's definitely a strong energy, anger. And yet, not real for some reason. The stuff got wet, so what?

"Tried" to get into an Ayahuasca trance state, while assisting at ceremony without participating with the medicine, but I couldn't. When I stopped trying, there was only sweet joy. I did not ask anything like I used to during former ceremonies, like why, what for, where to, how ... It was just some kind of trust and presence. There was only sweet joy. Just enjoyed the ceremony humming along to the songs, rocked like a baby, tapped feet on the ground, had fun. Wow! Sweet.

After ceremony Freddy called me over. He needed me now, he said. He cried, sharing his experience with me. He now understood, got the message about the bullying issue he had been going through as a teenager, he said. He felt compassion. For the guy who bullied him. He could feel him. He could feel his pain. He could understand his problems. He felt what that guy felt. And he was moved deeply. He was very moved, cried, and was happy to have found the answer to his burning childhood issue. No more ceremony for him. No more need.

I feel blessed. I feel blessed for all those people opening up to me. For having had the chance to be there when they needed someone. For having been given the trust and confidence by so many people, to share their most intimate fears and stories. To being open to me, becoming vulnerable and naked. To learn. Thank you.

16 - A Week in Punta Hermosa

Traveling Deeper without Moving

When I had the urge to travel a few weeks ago, I had gone to Iquitos to an Internet café to get a flight to anywhere. That day, the Internet didn't work properly and there were no decent flights that would have been somehow interesting for me. That day everything kind of went wrong. Or, in other words, everything worked its own way. So I just went back to the jungle.

The morning after the ceremony I went to breakfast at 10:30. Pascal said: I'm going to the beach, surfing. Want to come? We leave at 11.

Shoot, I thought to myself, that's exactly what I want and said: let me have some breakfast, then I will tell you. As soon as I had taken the first bite, I knew I wanted to go. So I packed some sandwiches, ran back to my house, and packed my backpack. Just made it for the boat to leave. Allison came as well. It was good for her, too, to get out and get some distance and clarity.

Arriving in Iquitos, we went straight to the Internet shop and started looking for tickets for the three of us. We found a decent flight to Lima that we could still make, but the online credit card system didn't work properly. So we took a moto-car and headed to the airline's office downtown Iquitos. We got our tickets and went straight to the airport. Hurray. This time it worked out.

Pascal had been working in Lima with Cirque du Soleil for half a year and knew the city. We stayed in a beautiful colonial style hotel in a hip area and shared a three-bed room. It was fun and very interesting to go back to civilization after being a long time in the jungle.

16 - A Week in Punta Hermosa

I reflected. At the retreat center there were always people and we shared breakfast and lunch every day. People shared their experiences, what they had lived during ceremony, where they came from, what they did for a living, and how they saw themselves. And the managers would share their opinion, talk about the power of Ayahuasca and how they thought the messages they got should be interpreted. I stopped interacting in these talks unless I was asked. Those chats were not helpful, I felt. For me it was important to give people the chance to find out for themselves. What did it really mean for them, in their personal situation, whatever they had experienced at night with the shamans. I wouldn't withhold my stories, but I wanted to make sure not to influence those people who arrived newly at the retreat center with my Ayahuasca experiences.

Reason being is that people start comparing their own experiences with others and then judge it good or bad. That doesn't work. As the shamans had told the manager couple: they needed to find out themselves what it meant for them. Both had seen a different version of separating. She saw they couldn't have babies and therefore would separate. He saw another highly interesting lady that would show up at the retreat center and that would be his true love. She couldn't have children and therefore shouldn't continue together. Two stories with the same outcome. Separation.

The shamans said the messages needed to be translated, you couldn't take them all direct. Like I had seen a scary-looking ugly face of a wild-looking man in my belly, once. Another time I saw myself as an embryo in my own belly. Another time I felt as if a comb was straightening out the inside of my brains. Or, my crown chakra being on fire and actually hurting like hell. Obviously, you can't take that picture as a direct message.

So the young couple was faced with the idea of separation. Instead of using that picture to reflect on what that meant for them, they thought they should separate. "Mother Ayahuasca had told them ..."

What did they really want their relationship to be like? How did they feel about it and what made this picture show up in the first place? They just decided that's it. They said they discussed a lot. But doing Ayahuasca two out of three days and running a retreat center doesn't leave much quiet time, time without being in trance tripping, to actually

Headless Chicken

face the situation and go deeper in the here and now. Maybe they did look deeper and needed Mother Ayahuasca to dare to be truthful. As far as I understood the whole shamanic work and healing processes, all that happens is that you start opening up to your true self and then healing can occur. In other words, ego is being overcome temporarily and the truth can show up.

I feel whatever shows up is a part of oneself, or of something we are connected to. One big truth. For me it was absolutely important to integrate those insights in my everyday state of being. It is not enough to trip and see and hear some great stuff. I want to be responsible, able to interact responsibly, not being a victim. Do my part. Live my part. Acknowledge my part. No longer use external factors or situations to excuse whatever was happening, like a victim. I create what I live. And I can heal.

Every dis-ease has a reason to be, some kind of origin and a higher purpose why the original issue effects as a disease. The purpose is to shake us a bit, to wake up and question if we are still on our path or if we got distracted, manipulated and consumed.

That message that the couple got, to separate, in my eyes was the very deep issue that comes from inside and was already there before taking Ayahuasca. I feel it is important to acknowledge that, be honest, and be okay with it, not make it a hallucinating drug's issue, Mother Ayahuasca responsibility.

The two of them were in a critical state physically and mentally and it was great that Allison took the chance to get out of the environment with us for a week. And also to take a week off "working with Ayahuasca."

We had a hilarious time strolling up and down the streets of Lima, visiting hippie markets, veggie cafés, seeing street artists, talking to strangers, floating from one situation to the next. Allison had a tarot card reading done and I translated. I must admit, I added some neutralizing words to each phrase, so this could be understood in various ways and you had to figure it out yourself. Allison was very easily influenced. Too open. Pascal and I both felt she could use our care now. So the three of us just had an easy time, while inside of us a lot of things were moving.

16 - A Week in Punta Hermosa

Some jewelry maker gave me a beautiful necklace made from a seashell as a gift. Pascal said he knew him from a few years back when he lived here. I was touched and very happy to receive a gift out of the blue from someone who didn't even know me.

The next day we moved on to Lima Beach and stayed at a place called Las Hamacas, "the Hammocks." We shared a bungalow right on the beach on the Pacific Ocean. It was a bit fresh and not possible for us to surf, due to the strong current. To get into the sea past the big waves looked dangerous and challenging. I had several injuries from outdoor sports, for not really being responsible. Last time in Lake Tahoe snowboarding, I had followed a bunch of very advanced snowboarders cross country in deep powder. I thought, if I just follow and do what they do, I'd be fine. Fear is just an illusion in the mind and not real. That's what I thought. So I tried to just think differently and forget about the fear. Unfortunately, I wasn't as advanced of a snowboarder as they were and didn't consider that fact at all. Well, powder is soft anyway, I thought. I remember the tree I hit for not being able to ride as fast and as accurately as they did.

A very hard branch ripped open my cheek and left a long, deep bloody wound on the face. But the real problem was that the inside of the cheek was torn apart. A lot of blood was gushing out. The snow made it look even worse. I went to the hospital, they wanted to give me six stitches, but I decided to let it heal by itself. The hospital visit cost me 600 bucks. I wondered how people can afford that.

So that's why in Peru I decided not to surf. It was just not the right conditions for a humble beginner. And I didn't want to force anything and risk too much. Not only did I not have insurance, I was also far away from the shamans.

Surfing had been the only idea I came up with, a what to do before I die. At the time I was faced with stage 4 malignant melanoma, possibly dying within the next week in the year 2000. All of the big dreams of changing the world and developing some kind of project to help humanity get better had been blown away quickly. There was possibly, hardly any time left to live. Actually, surfing was what my mind came up with, an exciting idea. I always wanted to do this after trying once. But then, when I had the official cancer diagnosis in my hands, even my big dream of surfing wasn't important anymore. All that counted was here and now. And somehow, I realized at that time, I didn't even want to live anymore. Ouch. Nasty. My only problem to die had been that I would leave two children without a mother. That was my only problem why dying was not an option. I didn't really care about my own life. That realization was shocking. Looking back, there had been so much sadness, trauma and struggling. I had lived other people's lives. Especially the last few years before cancer. But also before. I tried hard to figure out things, but just didn't realize that my perception of myself was not who I really was. My main concern in life was making sure not to harm anybody and doing the right thing. But I hadn't lived from my own center, but from thinking. And that had been a consequence of what I had been told and exposed to. I had to go so far to finally realize that what I thought I *should* do in life was nothing, but what I *thought I was expected* to do for others. Complying with expectations instead of living your mission. And even these expectations were a mental interpretation of my mind. I had created my world without bothering to include myself in it. My true being. I had attracted people that cared for how I showed up, what I achieved and how I would fit in into their world. And I did. I have been a specialist in adapting to any situation. I had disciplined myself in such a way that I just closed my eyes and did what I thought I had to do without caring too much about my heart. As if there was no center and no bit of Manuela left.

After all this hard work, without daring to feel myself and find out that I had put myself in a dead-end road, I thought at that time. After all this painful journey of burnout, lack of vision, lack of hope, lack of motivation, having had the guts to leave an ended relationship, business, money and security in order to live more truthfully. Starting from zero as a single mom with two kids. Now this? All that struggle for now dying? Where was the point?

I never died! After five years of quarterly checkups inside out and upside down, I had been free of malignant melanomas. The cancer had done its job: awakening me from the illusion of being alive and living the life of others, versus creating life.

So there on the beach in Lima it wasn't a big deal for me that what I was looking forward to most, surfing, wouldn't happen. I could easily let go.

16 - A Week in Punta Hermosa

There was a slackline right in front of our bungalow to balance on. Cool! Something else I had been interested in. It was so revealing to observe body and mind. At first, I was swinging big time very quickly from side to side. As soon as someone offered me just the tip of the finger to connect with, something inside of me developed a kind of stamina as if I now allow myself to believe you can do this! Then, it became very obvious how the quality of my thoughts would impact the outcome of my performance directly.

Only very few times I managed to look at the other side of the line and just walk there as if it was the most normal thing to do. In those few times, there were no interfering thoughts. My mind was empty. All the other times, as soon as some kind of critical thoughts came up, the body started shaking. Wow! What a direct answer. Not your wish is my desire, but, your thought is. What you think is what you get. Clearly. And in this case immediately.

Allison took classes of tai boxing on the beach. It was great to have that opportunity to be right there. To do something that connected her with her emotions and with her body.

I used to walk along the long coastline for hours. My remedy of walking meditation to get back to myself from thinking. It was very interesting how being back in the "regular world" seemed to impact the quality of my thoughts and triggered emotions. Victimized. Instead of judging myself or my ego, I could just watch and let go. It felt like in a nowhere space. Kind of unreal. Everybody smoked pot around here except me.

I had only smoked a few times in my whole life. As a teenager I felt dizzy and sick. Everything other than a pleasant experience. So I didn't do it again. Then, in Lake Tahoe, one morning, without thinking, I took a couple of strong drags of the pipe as if it was the most normal thing for me to do. It was at 2500 m altitude, before breakfast. It must have been some very potent stuff, as I immediately lost vision, saw only dots. Then lost hearing, as if I was in a totally soundproof environment. Then my heart started beating faster and faster and I couldn't breathe any longer, couldn't get any more air into my lungs. Then I fainted. I saw from a different perspective how my former partner was dragging me into bed. Connection to body, mind and sensation was gone. And yet, I noticed everything. I still had thoughts.

Headless Chicken

Gosh, I thought, now you really messed it up! You die for smoking pot! The kids are not small anymore but you don't want to do this to them, leaving them without their mom. Horrible ... so I struggled to get air and was in panic. Until my partner said, "Relax. It's okay." So I did. Then, I was really gone. I had let go. I could see everything from above. I saw myself lying in bed. I saw my partner first leaning over me. Later I saw him as a ten-year-old standing in the corner. Interestingly enough, I did not know at the time how he looked as a ten-year-old. Only later I found out that the photos of him as a child matched with what I saw. Freaky. Then I saw a big black void kind of tunnel, as if the black in the center was even more intense black than the surrounding black. It was going away from me. Or maybe coming toward me? And I was traveling it. Then, I saw my whole life passing backward in seconds like a hologram: Picture of the face, state of being, situation. The situations were rather dramatic and sad. But when I witnessed it, there was no sadness. It just was. And I was some kind of entity seeing everything. A bunch of all there is, total peace, no mind, no body, just a witness in the vast, unknown, safe space.

I don't remember how long I had been gone. Just that they were going to call emergency. But then I came back. It took me a few months to digest the incident. I never smoked again and I sure had lost the last bit of fear of death. I figured dying might be uncomfortable but being dead is really a great place to be. I remembered how I never really wanted to live. I never admitted it, not even to myself. That's why I stopped eating when I was young and had to have cancer, to realize who I really was, to hold on and question what I was here for. To wake up from the illusion. To start living my life, allowing life to happen and co-creating life on earth together with the others.

After all that, what else could happen, really? I am already safe. Because I know I am conscious. I know without thinking. It is just there.

Yet, there was still some ego stuff to be cleared out to do with sex and money. I guess once all the old stuff is cleared out, you have got to constantly clear out new stuff. Like cleaning the house.

Now, I slowly got the hang of how to do this. And there on the beach in Lima was the perfect place to do it: Acknowledge what bugs you, allow yourself to look at your thoughts, emotions, triggers that have been pushed. Be okay with that (no judging), forgive whatever happened to

16 - A Week in Punta Hermosa

whoever. For me that person I needed to forgive first was myself.

There were very few people I had blamed for their behavior, since I had been looking at them through the glasses of their ego and thought that was compassion. That had nothing to do with compassion. Understanding, yes. But only head, not heart. I had to forgive myself, because I didn't live up to my own needs and desires. I excused others and judged myself wrong in any situation. I neglected myself and allowed myself to stick around people who did what was not okay with me. All silently. I created my own prison in my mind without noticing the prison in the first place.

All it would have taken would have been talking my truth. And then acting upon it. But how to do that when you are disconnected, you can read books. But that's just accumulating information on the hard drive. To be able to use that knowledge it has to be lived, to become a part of you. You need to establish or remember that most important relationship to your inner self or higher self. That last step of truly saying yes to the relationship to ourselves. To feel it, to feel us. Otherwise, it's just a farce, mental acrobatics, like reading the Bible to work your way up to a higher grade. It takes that quiet exploration time regularly, where you connect with that deeper part of yourself, beyond thinking, beyond ego.

February 12, 2015

Had a funky mind yesterday. OK, I get it. The monkey stays alive. Even if you know it is unreal and programmed, junk mostly. Was peaceful and then the memory of "should I" appeared.

Should I plan my life? Should I really know in my box mind the next step? Do I need a concrete long-term goal? Deep down I know how it works: deep down there is a connection to something that is bigger than yourself. And that big thing includes all there is. You are part of it. If you keep on limiting yourself to your local hard drive, you work separately from all there is and what you would determine as your goals, plans, and steps were ridiculous miniature versions of what is possible, mostly based on the information somebody else has saved on your hard drive.

The really important stuff doesn't work like that. For that, you really need to let go.

So I allowed myself to let go and be in this trancy, meditative state of ease and grace. Dare to experiment! Today, I got the answer again: whenever your mind tries to complicate your life and makes you suffer, remember who you are! Close that Mula Bandha (body lock in yoga) at the bottom, lift the energy slowly all the way up and open the crown chakra. Focus on Ajna, the third eye. Feel, sense your essence, just like you do when you work with clients. I could feel them, now I could focus and feel myself. Be good to yourself. Remember who you are. From there, you can ask your higher self questions like: What do you really want?

So I go ahead and experiment with that brand-new kind of channeled meditation technique. Today, I got one answer: Summer in Europe at this point, winter in a warm place. South America feels great. Just do things you are attracted to. Coaching, acting, exploring something new with like-minded people, develop something together, whatever. Appreciate the moment!

Thinking of corporate coaching and Pascal's business project in Santiago de Chile. He had invited to me to come along with him and cooperate. He wanted to form a team and experiment with co-creating. Therefore he wanted me to come to Chile with him for a month or so. Even though I really liked him and trusted him, it didn't feel right. I had absolutely nothing on the map and I was thrilled to have that opportunity and yet it didn't feel quite right. So I didn't go for it.

That day, I dream a bit. Whatever feels good, I hang out with and visualize, play, just dream. Thanks.

Dreaming had become an important part of my life. Whereas before, I always tried to keep the feet on the ground, don't float away, and be realistic. Without a trance-like state of nonthinking no major innovation. Without dreaming we can

16 - A Week in Punta Hermosa

just copy something that's already been done and possibly make it better. Without dreaming, no real innovations. Without dreaming much less visions of possibilities. Dreaming is the state where we allow new thoughts to come in. Thoughts that have not been proved. Thoughts that might sound ridiculous to the box thinking mind. Dreaming is essential for development, expansion. At least for me.

The week passes quickly. And soon we are back in the luscious green of the jungle.

* * *

Later on that year, I am actually booked as a business coach in Europe to work for groups of managers and executives for creativity, team building and leadership trainings. I became very creative, mixing improv games with what I heard in Ayahuasca. I don't think I would have had the guts to do the kind of experiments I did before. It takes total trust and fearlessness in the process to work.

17 - "Final" Insights

Last Weeks in the Jungle

Amazing how we can ignore our own wisdom and intuition. Amazing how the ego can twist and bend any circumstances into something else. Reinterpret. Amazing how easy it can be to remember who you are, and listen to that inner voice. And then forget again, listen to the ego voice, doubt, let the old program take over until you remember again …

After we came back from the coast, Pascal leaves a few days later. I clearly know it is the right decision at this point not to go to Chile for that business project. Even though my mind can paint nice pictures, thinking of the possibilities. My guts say something else. I can feel the difference between intuition and ego right now. What a blessing. Having your compass right there all the time. And allowing the chatter in the mind to be, to turn down the volume and to shut up eventually and then, tune in and feel …

> Ayahuasca 16
>
> Don't remember what made me continue going back to Ayahuasca ceremonies. I guess that is the part that people say can be addictive. You want to know more. Originally Ayahuasca was not meant to be a regular thing to do, other than for shamans. This is dangerous. Never know enough …
>
> Message: accept all of yourself, not only what you judge as nice. It needs to be truly accepted first, before you can let it go. Love yourself.
>
> Acknowledge all sensations, feelings, emotions, thoughts.

17 - "Final" Insights

"How do you feel?"
"What do you think?"

You have been given emotions as your guiding system, a sophisticated language between soul and body. Dare to feel! Any feeling is just as good. Anger, fear, sadness, joy. By feeling, you read your inner compass. That's about it.

Ayahuasca 17

Francisco's mother, who is also a shaman, is visiting. They both sing during the ceremony. For me, the big experience comes after ceremony. Everybody had been leaving the ceremony, Don José and all the guests. It was way after midnight. We had started at 8. Also the managers had gone home. It must have been almost morning, only Doris was still around. I still shared house with her. That special location in the middle of the hall right in front of the shamans, she had been assigned to special treatment. I would have never thought that was useful, but what do I know. The shamans said that makes her feel more secure. It could have increased the notion that something is really wrong with her, that's why she is not in line with everybody else. Oh well ...

There in the center, she had set up her own special extra equipment that she had brought along. A personal extra mini-ceremony within the ceremony. Yes, kind of separate, even though the idea was to put her in the center ...

The two of them, Francisco and his mom, called me over. There is just the three of us, Doris and the guide left. There always had to be a guide to make sure everybody got back to their home in the rain forest after taking shamanic medicine in the middle of the night.

Somehow, it was a very special moment.

During ceremony something said: Heal the source of your problems! Makes sense. What is the source?

Headless Chicken

After ceremony, Francisco's mom keeps on singing for me. I see a pretty much all gray childhood in detail. Gosh, I really hope the rest of the family didn't have the same nasty, sad experience as I did all those years. I not only see but experience and feel some kind of dull numbness. Wow, another big-time trauma relief. Who would have guessed, there is yet more to be healed …

I see both parents in distress, unhappy, sick. Hear myself praying the good night's prayer: "Dear God, please let Mommy get healthy!" Don't recall my mother being sick, but do recall that I always asked God to make her healthy. Maybe, I just meant God may make her happy. She was working in our shop, interior design. He was out, working at clients' houses. We lived at my grandparents' house, his parents' house. In the same grounds were also the shop and his workshop in the same big historic building. The business was run by the family, third generation already. Formerly a saddle maker, then a furniture maker, then an interior design shop.

My granny was always there. That was my dad's mom. She always had the last word. My mom didn't feel happy. She was uneasy. Whenever she could, she would take her three children, my brothers and I, and walk over to her mother's house to get a break from the prison she felt she lived in. I had learned by copying. I judged emotions into good and bad. Obviously, only the good ones could stay and the other ones had to disappear somehow. That was part of the education. Neglect, suppress, distract, fake and perform, ignore and forget. That was about the range. And I had learned that very early and really well too. Thinking about the sexual abuse that I forgot at age six and then remembered at age thirty-three.

I had learned that so-called negative emotions such as anger, fear and sadness are not allowed to be shown, but be suppressed. That was what I had learned, with the promise to be loved, to be considered a good girl, or a good person. Only show the good. Do not share the rest of the truth! That's how I learned to address my anger inward against myself. Hiding. That's how I learned to swallow my tears. That's how I learned to ignore my fears. Build walls, walls of my own prison.

17 - "Final" Insights

In the environment where I grew up, there was not much time and energy to give much attention and space for tender loving care to the kids. Two distressed people, shut up and disconnected, in emotional chaos. He depressed, she probably as well. You can only give what you have. They have not been able to give it to themselves at that time: Love.

I see three young kids in the little box. They are precious. That must be the tiny bedroom my brothers had a bunk bed in. My bed was at the foot of my parents' bed in the master bedroom. The situation is very sad. But now, I think it wasn't really, that's only how I felt, I could feel the others. They were not happy, that's all.

Then, Dad passes away, out of the blue. It was not fun before, yet, I got used to endless void after. Emptiness, lack, nobody and really nobody to lean on, to talk to, or be hugged. Felt left behind. Freaking alone. Huge cold space. Before and after his death. Just now, after he had gone, more obvious. Also, I grew and learned to judge. Through all of that, I naturally learned to look for the light. I needed to search and find. Create my own world. Be in my dream world with the Barbie dolls. Create how it can be. Have them interact differently from what I had known. Communicate, tell the truth and share whatever was really going on. I didn't care for the clothes and looks of the dolls. They could communicate freely. I just loved them interacting with each other. All by myself. They had all possibilities! They could choose! They were free! They were my hope.

Funny enough Lucy, the cook, used to call me "La Barbie" ...

I see myself as a kid, hanging out in the trees behind the house, my sanctuary. Outside being with the trees felt like home. That was my world, my joy, where I was really at home. What a gift! The source of the problems, negativity from generations, shame and guilt, was draining energy from my parents and to me. That's what I needed to heal. The source, the cause. Not the situation, but my response to it. That's what I needed to gain back, my own power to respond freely.

Headless Chicken

I guess at the time the idea was to be a good girl to be loved, try to make them suffer less. See them happy. And healthy. Automatically, I did that, obviously not consciously. That kind of suppressed energy I was exposed to and absorbed most of the time. I had not realized the difference between them and me. That's what kids do when they are little. Copy them. Until today. But not any longer.

I had been like codependent. Suffered from their suffering. Yes, I remember wishing: if only she (my mom) could be happy, then I could relax and be happy too.

It is all about the attention, what you focus on. It's not only okay, but necessary to focus inside first. Center! What is going on inside of yourself? Even ego is okay. Acknowledge, accept, agree. It is part of you. Allow it all to be there in this very moment. Don't think it away! Then, only then, choose how you decide to respond. You are not in a prison. This prison is an illusion. Don't attach to desires, likes, dislikes. You are here to fulfill wishes, without any attachment. This is like a movie. One scene is over, next comes. Done, past, yesterday. Next page. You write the screenplay. You direct it. You play it. Don't get stuck with it. Everything is temporary. Just live it, learn from it and grow. That's the human experience. No more neglecting, ignoring, closing eyes. It's okay to have your own opinion and to share it. It is necessary to be yourself and show up as yourself, not as a copy, not as a mere heritage, but an individual soul.

It's okay to have egotistical thoughts and feelings. For you and everybody else. What counts is what you do with it. That's a tough one to get …

How you show up in the world counts. Just feel whatever is and then decide how you want to deal with it. It's okay to share your truth, even though others might not like it. Share yourself, don't attempt to change anybody, but be honest. Don't tell your opinion unless asked for or invited; in other words, don't impose your ideas! Sometimes messages may hurt others. Do not hurt others, yet know when you need to tell the truth. Even though it might hurt, it is better to talk the truth

17 - "Final" Insights

than withholding the opportunity for others to expand their limitations, free themselves from ego stuff that's not beneficial for anyone, but makes them stuck. You know exactly when and what. Your intuition is spot on. The only issue is to shut off thinking and start listening. Listen to the guts and heart. Clear out the noise. That's the only issue. Master that mind. Tame the monkey. Be the rider of the horse. First acknowledge and see it, you are good at that one, maybe too intense at times. And then accept it, do not ignore, resist or fight it. Resist the resistance. Then agree with it, say: it's okay. It is what it is. Nothing else. A scene of a movie. For me to learn.

When Francisco's mom sings after the ceremony, I feel I am that young girl again. All of a sudden, I can totally allow myself to feel the deep sadness, anger and fear. Memories were stored in the brain for me, like pictures. But now I was feeling the memory. Uff, so much energy running through my system. Never before could I really cry the tears that I had suppressed all my childhood. What a relief! Now, I became aware of suppressing my emotions long term, during and since my childhood. Lid dropped. Intense!

At what age does a human being create their identity? I am asking myself.

You don't need a father or mother role model in order to learn how to feel. Feelings and sensations are there anyway. Even though you might not have had any role models for learning how to express them. A dysfunctional, passively communicating family still has all the feelings, even if they don't show them.

You don't need to learn feelings, only how to express them. No need to learn them, work on them, fake them, imagine them. Just allow yourself to feel them, pay attention inside and they are there for sure. I feel healed. More healing has occurred. This whole identity illusion has drifted away. I am no longer the idea of the consequence of my parents' behavior, the idea of a messed-up childhood, the idea of being incomplete, or not being good enough. I have everything!

Last message that night: you know and have it all.

With that, I can relax. No more searching. Trust. Accept the gift.

Headless Chicken

The next day after breakfast I hang out with Lucy and the other kitchen helpers, the lady from Tamshiyacu who had started to work there a few days ago before I had left for Lima.

The three of us and Berna, the lady that washes laundry all day long every day, had been meeting around usually six just before sunset on the river. The atmosphere was spectacular. Lush green all over, the very wide river swirling its way toward Brazil with a special light. Sometimes the current was so strong that I became slightly scared whether I could swim or not. I am a pretty strong and safe swimmer. Worst case, if you drifted away you can always get back on the land somewhere and find your way back, I thought.

Berna had asked me if I was afraid. "Afraid of what?" I asked. "Of the boa constrictors," she replied. I laughed. Obviously in the jungle there might be boas. "No, I am not afraid," I answered. I didn't even know that there were boas in the river.

I was wondering if I was too careless or irresponsible and if I should stop swimming in the river. But my logical mind said that the chances of being killed by a boa is probably less than being run over by a school bus back home. Well, I had no statistics, it was just an assumption. So I decided to keep on swimming in the river. The only thing I was aware of was getting some kind of parasites I had heard of. So I made sure not to swallow any water. Also, someone said, "You better don't pee in the river, since those parasites can come up the urinary canal." Yuck.

The new girl at the kitchen had two small kids and lived just twenty minutes up the river. She was with us all week. Only on Sundays she would spend a couple of hours with her family, like Berna did.

The three girls and I had made friends. They called me "La Barbie" and I found that quite sweet. I took it as a compliment. Our conversations were simple and pretty touching. I guess we spoke more about what we had done in life, or what we had achieved, where we worked or what we could afford with the money we made. We talked about what was important to us. More about the here and now. Our dreams, beliefs, priorities and values in life and about what really is going on here and now. Lucy was very caring. She had cured my athlete's foot with special herbal baths during days and days. Wearing rubber boots in the heat and humidity of the jungle made it difficult to heal. You could

17 - "Final" Insights

feel her love. Berna was all happy because I gave her daughters a few T-shirts that I didn't need.

The new girl was a vivid, shiny, luscious lady, full of light. She loved to dress in strong colors, especially reds. That day, after breakfast she wore golden earrings with a red stone in the shape of a heart. "Qué bonito"—how beautiful, I said without thinking a thing. Instantly, she touched her ear and took off the earrings. "That's for you!" I was almost shocked. I couldn't accept that. That lady who works all week and hardly sees her family was going to give me her golden earrings? I looked at Lucy slightly worried what to do. Lucy said, "This is a gift that comes from the heart. You must not reject it." So I accepted. My heart felt like a river that was flooded. So much love. Later, my European brain kicked in, wondering what I can give her in exchange. But I knew deep down, this is not about exchanging. It is about giving and receiving. It was sure interesting to observe the mind going in circles searching for the adequate answer for this unexpected generous gift. I decided to wait and see if something that I would really like to give her would show up automatically. Or not. And it did eventually.

Interacting with these ladies gave me just as much insights as the work with the shamans did. These people live a very simple life and had hardly any possessions or "securities."

They did not worry about tomorrow or mourn about yesterday. They were fully present. And you could feel their heart. Well, I did. They could also be very spontaneous.
So one evening, Lucy tells me about the conversation she had with Jeremy. Even though she talked quietly, she was angry. And I could feel it. She had not been fully acknowledged nor rewarded for her constant extra input. She didn't get what she wanted. Weeks and weeks without a day off. And I believe she didn't refer to just money but recognition. I could feel her anger, even though she did not show it physically. The next day she was gone, together with Gumaro, her partner and lover. Without saying goodbye.

They were an interesting couple. I remember the day that Allison asked me whether I knew if they were a couple. Interesting, I thought. Who cares? They shared a house. Lucy was in her mid-forties and Gumaro twenty-one. One day Lucy told me their story. How they fell in love. How she thought about the age difference. How she realized

Headless Chicken

that it is not a problem for them, only for others. So from one day to another, they were both gone. And I missed them. Especially Lucy. And she didn't say goodbye ...

That "leaving without saying goodbye" had been a weak spot from childhood. My father disappearing (dying) spontaneously. Me not being able to say goodbye. They closed the coffin without allowing me to see him anymore.

Later in life, I had been seeing this charming and creative guy who turned out to be a drug addict. Not wanting to take on his drug problems, we had agreed on him not showing up at my house for a day or two after an intense cocaine night. The agreement didn't work. He still showed up and begged me to be with him. Despite being totally drugged. So I asked him to not show up for a few weeks. If I am not available he might possibly be motivated to get professional help. Suggesting that timeout, he immediately broke up with me. He never communicated with me again. That's when I remembered the old suffering from "leaving without saying goodbye."

The hardest lesson to learn about "leaving without saying goodbye" was four years earlier when my stepson had passed ... For the first time, after ten years of divorce from the kids' father, his girlfriend, his kids from his first marriage and last relationship, our kids and I celebrated Christmas together at his house. I could see and feel my stepson being disconnected and troubled. I just couldn't reach him.

We were sitting on the sofa, remembering old stories. When we drove to Austria in the tiny 2CV Citroen car, four kids and the Golden Retriever. When we were in Greece with the newborn baby sister, the first girl in the family and he had cut his little brother's hair pot-style. When we spent a summer vacation on the beach in Florida, him at age fifteen, his brother thirteen, their friend fourteen, my son five, and daughter three and me. How they managed somehow to buy a bunch of six-pack beers and got drunk in the pool house while I was cooking in the house. How we organized "Olympic Games" and his little brother accidentally kicked out his front tooth with his foot when he had lost the hundred-meter run. How we didn't worry because we knew Daddy was a dentist and he would fix it ...

17 - "Final" Insights

I could see there was something not right with him but I didn't know what. When I asked him, all he said was I just want to get over with my studies. "Getting over with" has a funky feel to it. I know that one. He had been studying medicine forever, finishing his high school after changing schools many times. He wasn't made for studying.

I didn't know about his private life. Once, he came for a vacation with a girlfriend to stay in our flat in Mallorca. But that relationship ended. I asked him about his cat and he said he had given her to the neighbors. She would be better off playing with the neighbors' kids. I got really worried. His beloved cat! At least he still had his dog. I just couldn't reach him.

After dinner he gave me a ride to the next subway station and I took off to my friend's house where I stayed. "Let's meet tomorrow, everybody, to watch a great movie together," I suggested before we went our separate ways. I thought the movie *Patch Adams* might reach him and move him. An inspirational movie with Robin Williams about a suicidal kid who discovers his mission to help people and become a doctor during a stay in psychiatry. He agreed to come and watch it with us. The next day we were at a friend's house altogether to watch the movie. Then I received a phone call that he couldn't make it.

A few days later they all left for a vacation to Israel. My ex, his girlfriend, my stepson and both of my kids.

On 3 January my daughter called me to tell me in a stammering voice: "Mommy, he is dead!" When I heard that message my head was about to explode or rip apart from the body, like a headless chicken: the body still works as usual, even though the head is gone. I felt like my heart had already exploded. Broken! I just couldn't cope, knowing that he wouldn't be coming back and that it couldn't be undone. I had no chance to change anything. Obviously not. Knowing that I couldn't protect my children from the trauma they had experienced, finding their brother dead in the bed next to them, killed me. I knew that I couldn't help. It was just too late. My mind was going wild to an extent that I was afraid I might go nuts. If he had seen the movie, maybe that would have helped, my thought went, etc., etc. ... That night I finished a bottle of hard liquor, more than half a liter. Better knocked-out drunk than getting crazy.

Headless Chicken

It took almost a week to get examinations and papers sorted, for them to come back with their deceased brother. I decided not to travel to Israel in my condition, but to sort myself out first so I could support the kids when they came back.

That was the most terrible situation I had ever experienced so far. I just couldn't accept he was dead. When they arrived at the airport with the coffin, they were devastated, paralyzed, traumatized.

Shortly after, he was buried in the family grave in the outskirts of Munich. The little chapel was packed with hundreds of kids, friends, all in their twenties. Some of them greeted me, asking whether I remembered them. I was just crying. It felt like all the tears that hadn't been cried many years ago and all the tears that were not cried by other people who would suppress them came out through my eyes. When the priest asked if anybody wanted to say something, I jumped up crying, to go to the lectern. My kids tried to hold me back but they couldn't. Even though I could hardly speak at all, because I couldn't control the tears, I looked into the crowd, and to the ceiling of the chapel as if he had been stuck up there in the sky and said: "All these people are here because they love you. I love you. I will always love you. You are not all gone. We stay connected ... "

It was all about love. That's all that counted. I couldn't reach him because he was under a veil. Drug problems. So he couldn't feel the love. I think that's what killed him.

It took almost a year to learn to accept and let go. My ego was going wild, holding on to an idea which wasn't true. How things should be, according to my understanding. For one year I couldn't look into somebody's eyes without getting tears in my eyes. I saw him in everybody, and it was too late. So I cried like a toddler whose beloved toy fell into the river, not knowing that the river leads into the big ocean. Until I understood and then I could accept.

So when Lucy left spontaneously, those old buttons were triggered. This time in a different way. Memories came up. Memories of situations, thoughts, emotions. But this time there was no automated emotional response. I would remember stories that crossed my mind, and I could accept that someone I cared for was gone and I might not see her again. It was absolutely okay. We had spent a beautiful time

17 - "Final" Insights

together, and we had appreciated it. The gift of friendship had been given. It's not to be possessed. Just to be enjoyed.

Seven months later, back in Majorca, I received a friendship request on Facebook from some stranger in Peru. She said she reached out to me to say hello from Lucy and Lucy sends her love!

Ayahuasca 18

Question: How do I manifest this change in the physical world so that it sticks? How can I make sure to live up to what I had learned, and live the knowledge, remember self-esteem, love, compassion, acceptance, agreeing versus resistance?

I still wanted to make sure that my mind was doing the right thing. Not quite what you would consider trust. Just still didn't trust my thoughts. I still wanted another confirmation that it would be good enough to listen to the heart. Again. Like as if it was never enough. Never enough confirmation. Ayahuasca had not given the ultimate answer.

The answer was abrupt and clear: Look at your fears! Fears are a guiding force. Look beyond! Find out what's behind, and get the answer. Fear is the opposite of love. Fear shows up because something wants to be unveiled: Love. That's the potential of change! Where there is love, there is no change needed. Where there is love, there is clarity and direction.

That night a lot of "crazy," unstructured movement is going on in the mind. Ayahuasca is processing. I feel it in the back of the head and the neck operating. As if I had tried to think feelings rather than feel them. The hardware seemed to be readjusted.

Acknowledge, accept, agree. Allow, let it be, whatever. First let it be so you get the message, the feeling. No more suppressing. Then you can let go immediately. You have to see what was there to be learned. Then make decisions how you respond.

Vision: The whole world is in your mind. It looks like I can see a miniature version of the universe in the center of my brain. Weird. But I can see it. Tiny. Like a drop. Don't know exactly if it is only in the center of my brain or in every cell. I see it in the center of the brain.

The next day that part of the head and neck feel sore. It doesn't really matter. I can cope with sickness and pain without suffering. Interesting. It really works: No judgment, no suffering. Isn't that easy?

There is this new French guy who suffered from OCD. I really don't know why they accepted him to do Ayahuasca. I wonder if the shamans we're totally informed and aware of the situation. I was under the impression that the medicine plant was not indicated in certain circumstances.

The day after his first ceremony he is totally disturbed.

And yet, he had hoped to find healing somewhere else. He didn't want to continue after his first Ayahuasca nightmare. I thought that was better anyway, but I am not the expert. He wanted to leave the retreat center, but didn't have any more money, since he had already paid for his whole stay, as everybody did, and had no extra money.

Unfortunately, the managers decided not to return his money and blamed it on Isabel's business policy. Ugly shit. So he stayed without taking Ayahuasca. Jeremy talked to convince him to continue the medicine. I don't remember if he did continue taking Ayahuasca or not, but he did go to ceremony, as far as I know without taking any more plant medicine. I had experienced that even though I didn't take any drugs, I could enter into an elevated state of mind, just being in the ceremony hall with the others.

That one night, I didn't go to ceremony, stayed home and meditated. Thank God! I went to bed early and slept really well. Until I hear someone calling my name in the middle of the night. Thank God, I was clear and cool about it. Had that happened when I first arrived here, I would have definitely freaked out, being all by myself in the middle of the jungle, in a house that did have a locked door, but no walls only fragile mosquito nets.

17 - "Final" Insights

As somebody called my name I could hear the French accent and knew who it was. I also knew about his condition. I was not afraid. There was absolutely no way I would not go downstairs and open up to let him in.

I didn't think he would break in through the mosquito nets, but I could not not help him and leave him in distress out there, totally lost in the jungle. He was in total despair. I could hear it in his voice. So I went down, and I opened the door and let him in. There was no light, since the generator was switched off some hours after the ceremony.

I lit a candle and offered him some water. That's all I had. He sat on my handmade chair. I sat on the edge of the little table. There was nothing else in the room. He talked. I listened. He explained what was going on in his brain. He was very wound up. His face looked pale and sweaty. He was a very healthy-looking guy in the first impression. Tall, skinny, black longish hair, glasses. I tried to follow what he was saying. I suppose it was around 3 o'clock that morning when he arrived. He talked and talked. All disturbed. Under serious stress. Fearful of his own mind. What a nightmare. Worse than a nightmare. Trying to find solutions with a mind that has some kind of a program error. He had gone back to ceremony that night and he had taken a small dose of Ayahuasca. He sure sounded like his mind was about to go nuts. But my feeling was, he had experienced that kind of mind fuck at other times as well. But now, it was obvious. At least for me. It was obvious that the stress he experienced was due to his mental interpretations of situations. Like everybody else, but harder and worse in his case. Even though he spoke very confused and unstructured, unclear, and wild, I wasn't afraid of the thought that he had gone nuts. He spoke like he had, weird but I felt, he just dared to express what was going on in his mind. Whereas in every day's life he wouldn't. Maybe there wouldn't be the right moment to share when such stressful thoughts appeared in his mind. Maybe there was nobody who would listen. Maybe there was just nobody who would understand. Nobody he could trust. He had been raised by his grandfather ...

He trusted me. And that night he needed me. I was glad I could be there for him.

However, after an hour or two, I stopped trying to understand and relate to what he was saying. I noticed how I got all consumed by putting myself into his skin, following his pathways of thoughts and conclusions. It cost so much energy. And it didn't really make much sense from my perspective. I had a feeling that the solution to the problem was not to be able to follow up on thinking patterns, but connecting to the heart so he could feel warmth and connection.

So I just sat and held his hand. For hours. It was important to stay in my own energy. Be the rock in the water.

To me it was obvious that the mind could create circles and circles of interpretations, assumptions, conclusions, distortions of perceptions and beliefs. All made up. Nothing real.

Two years later I learnt from my then mentor coach that this phenomenon is even known in the business world and explained by a loop of reactions called the "ladder of inference."

And yet for the owner of that mind it felt very real and his whole body response would act upon those made-up thoughts. So that guy, Jean Luc, suffered from not trusting his mind and having to check, confirm and make sure twice, thrice and more times that he had done what he needed to. There was just never an end to that not trusting. A constant fear. A constant tension. Never a break. I could certainly relate to that. Even though I could trust my mind, I always had been terrified to potentially do the wrong thing innocently and then become guilty. I had put loads of stress on myself for not trusting life, trusting nature, trusting God.

The common denominator was energy stuck in the mind, sucking up the energy needed to live fully, not just think, but feel, feel the heart. Connected.

Another long night. Different! But I felt so happy to be there. Just hanging out. Listening. Holding hand. No matter how crazy the stuff sounded he said, it didn't really matter. All that mattered was: he was not alone and I was where I needed to be.

When the sun came up at 7 o'clock I sent him home and went to sleep.

17 - "Final" Insights

Ayahuasca 19
February 21, 2015

Again, knowing there is no need for more healing right now, I go back to ceremony to squeeze out the job description. This desperate intellectual wish to find something, a word, a description and ideas that fit into the boxes we create. Only to find out the same thing that I knew before. Which is: You have no job description, no hat, no batch, no box. You are. That's all. You are them. You are all, the world is a reflection of your mind. Therefore, you create with your mind. Stop chasing jobs, titles, ego descriptions! Just be and be okay with it. Choose! Respond! The moment you manage to let go, dare to stop controlling the outcome and just trust, that moment miracles can happen and life shows up in the ways you couldn't even have imagined ...

How true. I had made that experience before. Moving to Spain with two small children who didn't speak Spanish wasn't the most logical thing to do for a single mom who just started her own coaching business. But I could feel it was the right thing to do. I felt it in the heart. That's why I had to stop thinking. I didn't want to mess it up.

Right after the cancer, there was nothing much left I would be super scared of. What could be worse? What could be worse than not living your life? Once we had arrived in Mallorca things were not too easy, but I was confident. Kids had to change schools twice before they got a spot in the school we had chosen. Then my son had a lot of accidents. Even before in Munich. Accidents ending in the emergency room: hit by a car, bloody cut on the lower arm from an exploding bottle, fainting when removing stitches and ending up in coma. Everything worked out fine at the end. We just got stronger and I learned to listen, trust and pray. Even though the first few years every winter I fell back into the modes of worrying about work when there was no work on the island. Instead of just enjoying the time. When I had no work in the morning in the warmer months, I hung out all by myself on the coast, listening to the waves. I remember I had to discipline myself to allow me to do so. How ridiculous. But when I did, I started dreaming. I saw beautiful pictures, doing fun stuff.

Headless Chicken

Soon after, a little senior model career started out of the blue at age thirty-eight. I had so much fun and was always picked for jobs that I really enjoyed. Obviously, my look suited the jobs I liked. Or my being is what they wanted. How I enjoyed getting makeup done, getting dressed nicely, getting catered, talking to interesting people and taking some photos. How fun is that? But the real fun started with the first TV commercial. It was just hilarious. During the first commercial I had to disappear into the ground at the airport and then reappear from the lawn at the hotel pool, all dirty. I didn't quite catch the story but I sure enjoyed the amazing creativity and technical gigs the carpenters created to make this story happen. And it was really fun to watch, totally my thing. From there on I had caught fire with filming. And how it all started was: dreaming!

> Then I saw my mom appearing in my vision that night. Felt pride about my mom. Saw her when she was younger. She drove that cool sports car and loved to speed. She always said, nobody knew how it looked inside of her. And: "If you kids were not here, I would be no longer around." I sure loved the way she showed up in the world.

> Then the journey continues: The way to live is to take responsibility for yourself and allow others to be as they are. Do not interfere. Be truthful however. Accept them as they are. They are you. We are all the same in millions and billions of shapes. However you treat yourself is how you treat others and how you are treated. "Fixing" one's self is bullshit. Fixing others even more. Get rid of the layers and be yourself. No need to fix anything, you are already perfect. You come from the source and are pure consciousness, pure potential. Get rid of the layers, then you come back to the source. Just be yourself, not your stories! Nothing more. Be your self!

February 22, 2015

All day very sick. Nauseous, weak. Even after so many times my physical system still has trouble to get strength back. No tai chi, no yoga. Accept it. Surrender. Talk with Michael, the Hungarian Canadian, and Andrew, the Polish Canadian. Even though I feel sick I am very happy with who I am. No need to

17 - "Final" Insights

prove, compare, show, defend, impress. Feel very connected to all other people. Remember the part of last night's ceremony: proud of my super mommy. That feels so good. Love her strength, beauty, good heart, creativity, dedication and good intentions. Memory of when I was a small kid, that I had forgotten: I was proud of her, I not only loved her, but adored her.

This is what it takes to heal my relationship to my mom and to my own femininity: acknowledge, appreciate, accept, honor that you are a woman. Not just focus on what might be wrong. What could be really wrong anyway? In hindsight everything makes sense as if a higher intelligence was organizing billions of details and it all fits together and serves a higher purpose. At the end that higher purpose is always love. What looks hard to understand and to accept at all, has a deeper meaning and behind every intention is love.

My son, twenty-four, likes proof and science. He also likes to help people. So he studied to be a doctor of medicine. He doesn't relate to all that I am talking about. Is love the intelligent intention behind everything? What is Love anyway? Does it need scientific proof? Good point. The thinking mind is not the right device to relate to love. The heart is … . You can't wash laundry in the coffee machine.

My daughter, two years younger, never knew what job to go for. Just like me. And yet, she feels clearly. And she started not trusting any longer at some point, just like I didn't. And I know I can't make this happen for her, but pray and have faith and allow her to make her own experiences to heal.

I have a nap at five, wake up convinced it is the next morning, but it is only 6:30 PM. Still sick, burping like hell. I thought of going to ceremony, like Allison—just keep going, take advantage of Ayahuasca and keep working on yourself. But now, the messages I get are very clear: you are okay. You are just fine. You don't miss a thing. No need to work on yourself. Plenty good enough. No need to cure anymore right now. Perfect. Do not doubt any longer! Apply the knowledge you have and that has been confirmed by the plant's spirit. Stop having to prove yourself. Stop continuously looking for confirmations. Just be. Accept the gift.

Headless Chicken

So I stay home. All good. My job is no other than being myself.

That was my last ceremony. Finally. Loud and clear. At least for now in the Amazon. Who knows what comes up in the future. Right now I know everything I need to know, especially: forget knowing, start feeling. All I have to do is apply it. And I also know how to do this. Shut up the monkey mind and feel inside. All I have to do is to remember. And then remember to remember when things get ugly. Ha! That's my reminder: when things get ugly, it's a good moment to remember to stop thinking, start feeling who you really are. Great reminder! Then I can just be quiet and listen. That's all it takes. When I get wound up in thinking, I remember who I am, feel the energy, the loving intention behind everything. And then I can just be quiet and listen. Then I can find peace and harmony, beyond the chatter of the mind. That was what I had been longing for most, my true wish: Love, peace, ease and grace. Oneness. Just like I saw it in my first visit to the spirit world.

* * *

Days are quiet. People come, stay, share, go. By now I got to meet dozens of people. Awesome people. Awesome changes. I feel blessed. Some big waves, some small waves, waves. When those waves first arrive they are bigger, when they go, they are smaller or even flat. That's the state of peace and contentment. The Polish guy from Canada and his buddy: Great people to get to know. Great minds, great hearts. The couple from Chile. They had something funky going on. I decided not to be curious. He worked as a lawyer and she as an architect. I could feel them, their busy minds and their possibly numbed hearts.

* * *

Isn't that what happens a lot in our Western world? We make sure the head works perfectly and secretly seem to train ourselves not to get too involved with feelings. It seems to hinder our performance if we mess with feelings. So we learn to suppress when uncomfortable and call it inappropriate.

Then, we wonder when we get out of balance, trying to live from the head only.

17 - "Final" Insights

The couple from Santiago de Chile was somehow drawn to me. I just shared myself when we met at the center, without talking much (like I did before!!!) nor asking or trying to influence in anyway. Kind of natural gatherings without trying to get anywhere, for the sake of enjoying our company.

Soon, they both approached me. I had been showing up in both of their ceremonies, they said. Interesting, I thought. I hadn't gone to ceremony since sometime. I felt it was time to stay home and meditate. The very same night they both saw me talking to them during Ayahuasca ceremony. How bizarre! And something clicked inside of each of them.

So the next day, they were both particularly happy and approached me to share their insights. And I was the lucky one who seemed to have delivered the message. Funny!

Sometimes it really just takes being who you are. That's the best you can do. Maybe it's always like that.

When they left the jungle they gave me a special gift: a beautiful Jack knife made of stainless steel and wood. I took this to Machu Picchu a few weeks later and cut my fruit with it. Now I have it in the car and each time I use it, I feel love.

Then there was a couple from close to where I grew up in Germany. An oldish yoga guru and his girlfriend, a girl my age who seemed to have quite a tough time in ceremony. The guy wasn't really old, maybe just an old soul, or a little worn out from former escapades. Who knows. I really liked them. They didn't have to show off. They were humble and still shared what they had to say. We had some quite interesting talks. He told me I could take the rest of my mask off now. And he was right: no more need to be super kind, just not to be attacked and to be left in peace. I can just be honest and risk losing those friends who only like me when I suit them.

He shared yogic knowledge, part of which I had been introduced to by my guru in India in 2007. I was still in touch by email with my guru. That year, 2007, I had plans to visit a children's foster home and then hike the Himalayas. Arriving at the children's foster home in Andhra Pradesh, I found his ashram and started studying and

Headless Chicken

practicing intensively with him. Blow hiking in the Himalayas with all of the tourists! This is a real precious gift, to have found this guru, I decided. I stayed for five weeks, and never stopped practicing what I have learned ever since …

We talked about acknowledge, accept and agree. And about work: not searching for something new, but building on what you have learned and practiced. In his opinion one should not toss all the knowledge and experience one has collected so far. It is like a red line showing you the way. And built from there. Especially in your late forties, he said.

It made sense to me in the mind, but I would never limit myself on just doing what I have always been doing. They needed some growth. Expansion or depth. My red line had been publishing, which is basically sharing information; coaching, which is basically inspiring people to access information themselves; modeling, which is communicating with means of pictures; and acting, which is a bit of a mixture of all of it. When we first talked, I felt I had a different opinion than him, because I always looked for something new and I loved that. Later, I realized, my own red line and that I was absolutely fine with following up on it. I loved what I did and I was excited to learn more of it in a different way. I didn't have a proper job description anyway, doing a little bit of all and mixing it. Yet, my intention was clear: I wanted to inspire, share, playfully and with fun. Raise my own vibration and invite others to do the same. That's not really a profession, but a mission: Live what you believe in and share yourself with the world.

In all those weeks we did quite a few special rituals. The fire ceremony, cleansing flower baths, saunas. We visited the tribal community down the river a few times, where people were dressed in almost nothing and created the most beautiful jewelry out of seeds and whatever they found in the Amazon forest. There was a natural "piscina," a little lake, serving as a swimming pool for the locals. Looked quite dirty, but it was pretty clean. And the botanical gardens with a wide range of healing plants belonging to the retreat center. All could only be reached by boat. No streets anywhere close to the center. Sometimes we got local visitors at the retreat center: native people from other communities came in hand-crafted boats and offered their handicraft things to sell to the visitors.

After all these weeks I got to know some of these people and we hung out when they came to visit. Those moments were most precious to

17 - "Final" Insights

me, when you get to share with others, totally different sentient beings who are willing to share themselves honestly, truthfully, fearlessly.

My feeling is that the closer you get to the cities, the harder it is to find that kind of warm-hearted, generous and friendly people. Not that they wouldn't exist. They just don't stand out. It seems as if what we call Western civilization is exactly what impedes a high level of honesty, truthfulness and courage.

Why would it be harder in the Western civilization to stay true to yourself and truthful to others? Deep down we all want to belong to some kind of group, something bigger. Most of us don't want to live all alone. What is it that makes this Western world seem so harsh despite all the luxuries? Why do we have to fake, adapt, neglect, ignore in order to be accepted? What's the difference in the jungle? Why can they be themselves so easily and we are trapped in ideals, programs and illusions?

Those so-called primitive cultures seem to have it pretty clear: they are a tribe and everybody has their position. There is not much competition. Even though you must show what you can and earn your position. But at the end of the day it seems like people don't give too much about higher or lower. Also, they don't seem to thrive on accumulating possessions. At least as long as they are not exposed to the Western ideals. That helps. Or maybe their rivalries don't show to the eye of a foreigner.

※ ※ ※

Then one day I get a visit. I almost had forgotten about him coming to visit us when Dan, my former husband, arrived. And there he was. He said he wanted to experience shamanic ceremonies as well. I was pretty relaxed, despite the recent divorce via mail and never seeing him since.

I had separated from him kind of spontaneously. I just did not follow him when he went back to the US. I stayed in Mallorca. It clearly didn't feel right to go back. Once he had gone, I realized that I felt much more relaxed by myself and that I had put too much effort into fitting into his life, neglecting part of me. Even though he did his very best to make me feel comfortable and provide a comfortable life. It just

Headless Chicken

wasn't for me. I was missing something essential and didn't want to live that lifestyle. My life was more about simplicity. His life was more about success. We both believed in spirituality. That's what united us in the first place. Obviously, growing up in Southern California it doesn't make it easy to get rid of that American business ideal and showing up as successful, no matter what. When we first met, I thought we had a real big thing in common: spirituality.

Everybody is spiritual in my eyes today. But not everybody knows it. He did. That's what made me finally give it a try at first, after six months writing and phoning. That's how I got to live in the States, married the second time, in order to be able to stay there with him. He didn't want to marry. Nor did I. The other option was becoming a nanny for the dog or something. So I married him rather than be employed as a nanny for his dog in order to be legal. Clearly ego! Oh well. Then, after three years in Northern California we lived in Europe for nine months or so, but he didn't like it. It was too rustic for him where we lived in Mallorca.

When he left to go back, I didn't follow. That was it. But then, when I wanted to file for divorce, he was sad and disappointed. Maybe devastated, hopefully his ego more than his heart, since he felt he had invested so much in this relationship. And I figured he referred more to money than personal input, whatever that means.

And I had invested almost four years to find out that all I needed was acceptance of myself, be myself and stop trying to fit into other people's idea of their dream girl.

In those years in the States I read books about narcissism and codependency and went to specialist therapists, referred to by Dan. Even though I didn't feel I had any more problem with something that had occurred in the past, and I had addressed issues, forgiven and let go. I probably hadn't. So or so, it was interesting to dig in one more time to see what else could be wrong with me. And Dan showed me the way to do so. We had many terrific times, snowboarded almost six months out of the year, did a few trips to beautiful destinations, invited friends. Yet, it just wasn't for me. And I could've known after a few weeks had I not doubted myself. And yet, looking back, it was not wasted time at all. We had a lot of great times. And after all, every dull, stupid, boring, dark, low situation had an inspiring, intelligent,

17 - "Final" Insights

exciting, light and evolving part to it in hindsight.

When Dan arrived I showed him his house, a cabin a little further away from the center. By the time we arrived there, he had teardrops in his eyes, when handing the divorce papers over to me. He shared his feelings. All he had put into this relationship, and how he had been dropped by me, he felt. I was very calm. Everything was okay that afternoon in the jungle. No drama, no blaming, no need to be right.

He visited one ceremony and decided Ayahuasca was not for him. It didn't make any sense to him to put his body through such pain since he already knew what he knew and there was nothing new for him to discover. He had participated in a lot of workshops, traveled around the US with a guru, organizing spiritual gatherings and things like that.

For me, I also found that everything I learned in ceremony is like a confirmation of something that I already knew. And yet, for me, it was good to put myself into this extreme situation, let go of attachments and experience spirit directly, while in the body and thinking mind, even though physically harsh. And find out: you can get hooked on spiritual journeys like on other drugs!

Soon he decided to leave the jungle and explore the city of Iquitos. He asked me to come along and invited to me to show him around. I thought this would have been nice, but I did not want to risk that he might start all over again with asking why, trying to change my heart and mind to his liking. Finally I had been able to be clear and say what I wanted. He understood, accepted and I made sure he was not under the illusion of getting me back or something. So I decided to go along. We actually had a good time. It was really fun to stroll around and just live the moment without pondering about the past or the future. As long as we both accepted what was.

I bumped into people I had met before. Some film guys working on that documentary who wanted to interview me. I told them that if we bump into each other again, and we have time, we can do it. And we did a few days later.

There were a couple of mystical moments and synchronicity. Definitely fun! Until that one evening, when Dan had drunk a bit too much. He

Headless Chicken

just couldn't understand how I did not want to sleep with him after him giving me a great massage as a parting gift, something I hadn't experienced with him before. Just massaging for the sake of massaging. With no need for anything more to happen. Just for me to enjoy. He got really mad because I did not want to go any further and talked hash with me. Then I got mad for a change. Yes! Before I would have felt guilty of not complying with expectations and possibly or even probably having produced those expectations in him unconsciously. I kind of liked that feeling of anger. Finally! It felt like a strong energy. My energy. I was not afraid, nor freaking out. Yet, I spent half the night outdoors in the corridor, making sure I could just be by myself and nobody would bug me.

Soon after, he left to spend a couple of weeks in the sacred valley, Valle Sagrado near Cusco and visit Machu Picchu. Again, he invited me to come along, but I definitely didn't feel that was the right thing to do after that experience. So I said goodbye and went back to the jungle. And he left for Cusco.

I arranged to get the ride back in the boat together with new clients who had just arrived from the airport. Once arrived in the retreat center, I realized my time was over. It was time for me to leave.

The Australian couple had unofficially separated and both were in a critical state, mentally, emotionally and physically. They did no longer want to continue with Spanish lessons and the situation of hostility with the owner of the retreat became more and more complicated and intense.

While Jeremy was neglecting the fact that he actually had been fired and asked to leave within the next month, Allison had accepted the end of their relationship and went through a phase of mourning and figuring out what to do next. She was looking for answers from Ayahuasca, and day by day, she got weaker and weaker physically from the intense tripping.

That was dangerous, I thought. The Amazon master plant was said to be a healing plant not supposed to replace your true feelings nor free will. She was lost. Hurt and confused. She had given up everything in Australia to come to Peru with her husband. He had been there some time before to heal some mental health issue he had suffered from.

17 - "Final" Insights

Ayahuasca seemed to help, that's why they decided to go back to Peru and manage the retreat center. The idea was to fully heal themselves while learning shamanism and making some money for a living. What they had not considered was that managing the place, struggling with problems with the owner and intense tripping over a longer period of time consumed a lot of energy and strength.

In my opinion this remedy is not meant to replace your own willpower, but help you better understand what you think and feel and this way heal old wounds. Like the shaman said: you must learn to read the message. You can't take it all literally. Just like the Bible. You can't take it literally. That's why I find it makes it dangerous for Western people: we just want a quick-fix solution. Swallow the pill, drink a shot, just don't get bothered. But Ayahuasca makes us see what we are not used to perceiving beyond our senses. It helps us understand the bigger picture. It helps us understand how life works and that everything is energy. But it doesn't take over our human life in the physical body with all the free choices and responsibilities. We are still responsible and free to choose. No blaming Ayahuasca.

Allison booked a coaching session with me for before I leave the retreat center. At the end of this session she remembered that she can only find her answers inside of herself. And that she needed to be patient, to learn to listen inside, especially in a state of crisis. She understood and knew that she needed to give herself some time to digest and heal before making big decisions. She was okay financially and could afford taking some time off.

18 - Leaving the Retreat Center

Time to Keep Weaving the Big Net of This World

Since many weeks I got the same message: it's time to live! Apply what you have learned into daily life! It's not enough to do Ayahuasca trips. Not for you! You are supposed to use and apply the knowledge in the material world, go play, enjoy, create, manifest.

My job in the rain forest was over. I witnessed how dozens of people went through tremendous physical, emotional and mental challenges. I saw people heal. Others resisting to be healed. Others, just having a good time. Others, getting a confirmation of what they already knew, to remember who they are.

That confirmation is like a universal voice inside of us, each of us, that is saying the same thing to everybody: you know already. You always knew. You just forgot the truth. Your mind got blurred from all the chatter around and inside yourself. You forgot who you are. You tried to be what you thought you should be, not knowing that what you thought you should be is just an imprint of other people's ideas and opinions on your mind. But you can't live your life successfully following other people's ideas and opinions. You got to figure out your own soul plan. If you believe you are spiritual or not, it doesn't matter. The law works the same for everybody. You feel, then you think and figure out your path, not the other way around. As soon as you only live in the mind, your life experiences become dull. And you are the victim of your emotions, you create your own daily drama. You have it all! You just forgot how to use it. You have the power to create your own life, the way it works and suits you and others best. Deep down you find all the answers. Beyond the turmoil of thought and emotion you will remember. That's where we are all one. It's not a mental concept. You experience it in that state of peace and total relaxation. There is nothing else, but one. Nothing to strive for. Nothing to

18 - Leaving the Retreat Center

secure. Nothing to risk. Nothing to invest. Nothing to do. Nothing to change. Just pure being for the sake of enjoying. Yes! That easy! And whenever you hear your mind say: "yes but … "; "but I can't just … "; "what if … ?," blah blah blah; then be assured, you hear your ego mind trying to stay in control. Yes, it requires courage to break through old mental programs. Programs that have been inherited since centuries. It takes courage to start swimming without knowing the next shore. Letting go of programs that served to control, to be controlled, and to control others while being without a new program. No more hiding yourself! You are not the program. You cannot afford to live a program. You must live your life. There is nothing specific to reach, to go for, to fight, to achieve, other than what makes you feel your heart beat higher. As soon as you practice to listen, you will recognize the difference between hip ideas from the mind and trails guided by the heart. All you have to do is trust. No need for specific ceremonies, trips, drugs. All it takes is establishing your own way to tune in and listen inside. No need for Ayahuasca.

That all made sense for me. And yet, it sure takes courage to break through fears and ideas that have been installed in our minds for centuries. Religion, politics, television, brands, trends, economy, environment, social pressure, family, friends, education. Leave it all behind or aside and figure out what really suits you. I have been doing this before. After cancer. But it is not a one-time enterprise. It's a lifelong process. You need to stay awake!

Since I knew I had to leave, I did. I decided to stay a few weeks longer in Iquitos. There I rented a flat about forty-five minutes walking distance from the center. The flat was a "real" building, with proper walls, windows, roof and a door with a lock. It was the only building like that in this area, an area where streets were no longer paved. The first few days I was a little afraid coming to and going from the house. I was different, the only non-Peruvian. In the area everybody seemed poor in terms of possessions and quality of possessions. I was amazed how people lived in such poverty right next to "proper" houses, just a few blocks down the street toward the center. My house was the only house with real windows and even an A/C. I seemed to attract what I was afraid of. Usually I felt compassionate with any kind of people. But now, I felt my neighbors' looks, thoughts and feelings as rather critical ones. The way they treated me when I went to buy whatever was available in one of those one "room shops": I didn't feel quite

Headless Chicken

welcome. Almost in every street there was a little shop where someone had converted the room into a "business," selling maybe fifteen to thirty different items or less. Local fruits and vegetables. Basics that every household needs. Even though I didn't feel quite comfortable, I decided to get over it and just tune in, as if I was one of them. I started playing with the kids on the streets, greeting the people, whether or not they greeted me back. Another reason for my particular state of being much more careful than usual was the guy who rented the house to me. In fact, he was not the owner of the apartment, but his business partner who ran a local health food store on the boulevard of Iquitos. Weeks ago, I had already felt an urge to speak to the owner of that shop without knowing why. They sold all the local super foods such as Maca, Cacao, Lucuma and Camu-camu. Each time I had passed by that shop, the owner was not there. I always talked to a very nice Peruvian lady. She forwarded me his email and I contacted him, saying that I'm very interested in his business, even though I had no clue where I could go with that. Then one day, in fact, it was when I was in town with Dan, the two of us went for a smoothie at the health food store on the riverside and bumped into the bunch of film people again who wanted to interview us. And finally I got to meet the owner of the store. We ended up talking and talking. Then, later on when I was looking for a flat, he was back in the US for a few months and subleased his flat to me. His business partner, a Peruvian guy, was supposed to manage money and keys. So he did. He also gave me a lift to the place, to show me where it was and to clear the apartment from stuff and garbage the owner had left behind. During that meeting, the guy told me his whole story and I had an intense feeling that he was looking for something else. Some kind of release from his suffering. There was some kind of hope. Somebody who made him feel better. Despite the fact that I was a life coach, I decided not to become too friendly with the guy. That was a good move. Maybe the effect of my Ayahuasca healing. I had run into dangerous situations with men several times in my life. Now, I recognized immediately the potential complication. Whereas before, I only saw men as neutral humans, excluding the fact that they were the opposite sex, possibly looking for something else. I used to just fade out that aspect of a situation and brought myself into seriously dangerous situations. Somewhere far away from everywhere, alone with a guy I "trusted" on the way back from an excursion, he took a "short-cut" and tried to push me to have sex with him. He couldn't.

18 - Leaving the Retreat Center

Despite the fact that I was afraid to be in the apartment alone with this business partner guy who needed something, I was glad that I had learned to be cautious, not so ignorant, more aware of things. He told me not to leave the keys in the door-lock in the night. Somebody could break the glass door and turn the key around to enter the house. I thought he probably had a spare key and I didn't want to be surprised by him at night, so I still left the key inside the locked door.

And the guy did turn up out of the blue several times during my stay. I acted as if I was a tough, cold, rather intimidating German business woman to not show any weakness or fear. It worked to keep him at a distance.

And after a few days, I got used to living in a rather dangerous environment, with lots of drugs and alcohol and always looked out to be aware of any possible threat or danger. Made me feel like I was in command. Whatever could come up, I could respond adequately. So I could pass by drinking men sitting at every corner, staring at me, without any problem. And when I went into town I used to come back when there was already no light. The sun goes down early and this area of town has no streetlights ...

Dan was still in touch with me by email. He kept suggesting to come to Machu Picchu. Suddenly, all of this inner conflict about wanting to go, but not wanting to give the impression that there was any hope to fix our newly divorced marriage, was gone. All of a sudden I felt it was okay, and safe to go as long as I kept my communication very clear. So I did. I flew into Cusco via Lima and met up with Dan. We then drove to the sacred valley to a place called Ollantaytambo. The whole place was magical. The village, the hotel, the ambience. Even though it was a touristic place, it looked like the locals were still living their lives like centuries ago: very plain and simple. Many of them still wore traditional clothes and it didn't look like they dressed up as a tourist attraction. There was a little marketplace, where people sold what they grew locally. The variety was not wide but everything was very fresh. And very reasonable.

We shared a room, there was no problem at all to share a room. All the trouble we had gone through before was gone. Dan respected and accepted me with my feelings and wishes even though he wanted things to be different. I appreciated that. In fact, I was happy. Very

Headless Chicken

happy! Didn't have to be so complicated. In fact, it can be a lot of fun, as soon as we let go of expectations, ideas, desires and just live the moment. And that was definitely a great place to experience that.

One morning we got up really early and took the train to Machu Picchu. Dan had already purchased a ticket to go to Huayna Picchu, the mountain across from Machu Picchu. Huayna Picchu is supposed to be even more spectacular than Machu Picchu and it takes between forty-five minutes to an hour and a half to hike up there. Machu Picchu Mountain is much higher and takes longer—about three hours. When we got there, I could only get admission to climb Machu Picchu, which I wanted anyway. Visitors are limited on both mountains to preserve the place. By the time I got there, I only had one and a half hours left to speed up to Machu Picchu. After that time in the day no more visitors are allowed to go up, since they need them to be done at a specific time. I figured I'd do it anyway. Even though I was very weak physically, I went for it. After nineteen Ayahuasca ceremonies I had lost a lot of weight and had not been physically fit. My body was totally cleansed and kind of worn out. I just kept going as fast as I could. Up, up and up. Sometimes my mind kicked in with the idea that the body might collapse or something. But I decided to let go of the idea and rather listen to the body. The heart was pumping hard, but no problem! In one hour and twenty minutes I reached the top and felt blessed, as if I could embrace the whole world. The views were spectacular. But more than that was the feeling: I just felt free, light, spaceless, timeless, endless, one …

It was worth the effort. The sensation was priceless. Even though I couldn't stay long, I felt like this experience nobody and nothing can take away from me, it's part of me.

During that week in the sacred valley we did some nice trips to close-by villages, sacred sites, handicraft markets and manufacturing places. That was a truly unforgettable trip and I was very grateful and felt really blessed. Funny enough, well not really funny, we arrived a whole day late to Cusco airport. Our flight was a day earlier. That was the first of the free planes that I didn't make within the next few weeks! So we stayed another day in Cusco and left the next day for Lima. There, Dan took off for the US and I went back to Iquitos. That was the last time I saw him. A very nice memory and a beautiful way to say goodbye, farewell.

19 - Time to Move On

How to Transport the Knowledge Back Home

I stayed another week in Iquitos in my rental flat, met all people I had gotten to know, gotten to appreciate and given a place in my heart. It was as if I went out to say goodbye to everybody, except, it just happened without me planning to meet anybody. A perfect line-up of incidents. Sweet.

I visited the local hospital, because I had met a nurse who wanted to show me the local medical facilities. She was obviously proud of it. To me it looked rather like a junky place, I would have had more faith in the shaman's off grid than the hygiene at this place. Yet, they loved their hospital and were proud to have one. So I acknowledged.

I hung out for quite some time with some people in a hostel right on the plaza I resonated well with. Gosh, what a fun crowd of different people from all over the world. Obviously, one matter united us: we all believed or knew that we are spiritual beings and came to the jungle to remember and celebrate that. Some hippyish "alternative" people from the US and Europe, therapists, expats who started living a simple life in the Amazon, people who learned about shamanism, people who came to heal and were actually healed, people who like to be smoked all day, others who were rather down-to-earth despite the fact of being spiritual. People who explored. People who worked the ground. People who looked for something else, something more …

I was there due to a bizarre calling watching that YouTube video three months back. Even though I did not know why and how I should go there, I knew that I had to go. That knowing is a deep-down knowing, say beyond the stored data of the thinking mind, way beyond reason and logic. It just is. And it is strong. Beautiful.

Headless Chicken

At the end, I did do the interview for the documentary in a treehouse in the garden of the famous Fitzcarraldo movie location. That was one of those situations when it feels like something is talking through you, without you having to think, judge and edit before speaking. Due to this project I met more beautiful people from all over the world. We hung out for hours, sharing stuff. Therapists, alternative healers, artists, film crew, farmers, handicraft people, musicians, cooks, world travelers, spiritual people, all there to let go of ego and share their inherent beauty. That's how it felt. Obviously, that was my perspective. And I knew! What I seemed to witness was the mirror parts of myself that helped me become more aware. And it did. It became all so obvious that I could no longer deny seeing and understanding. All the things that I tried to explain to coaching clients before and the things I tried to figure out in my own life. The black spots that we just can't see through because of our filtering lenses.

Strolling through town a last time, passing through the junky areas toward that amazingly wild and weird market, where the vultures take care of the leftovers that everybody just tosses on the ground, I witness my inner world: as soon as a certain quality of thought kicks in, a certain quality of emotion and follow-up scenario appears. According to those thoughts, the movie is being pre-played in my mind, if I am not fully aware. I can get sad, depressed and fearful in a split second. And I can go peacefully and present, once I remember who I am, what I am. I witnessed a little made-up horror scenario in my mind. Obviously not purposely. Caused by the thought: What will come next once you go home, back to Mallorca? The typical rational thinking process kicked in:

You have to make up your mind to what you want to do.
You have to know what you want first of all.
You have to set a goal.
You have to plan steps.
You have to program everything.
And you have to follow up on the steps you have planned.

This little mental roller coaster drove me directly into an emotional roller coaster. In fact, I almost got trapped, stuck. Then, I remembered what I had learned: Open your crown chakra and look through your third eye, whatever that means. Basically, it means, stop thinking. Open up to that part of yourself that is bigger than your rational

19 - Time to Move On

mind, your body, your emotions and even bigger than yourself. It is like opening up the connecting device from my soul to the big spirit, the one. I had to experience this little crisis, which I witnessed many times afterward, again and again. In other words, the ego hasn't died, but it is being put into its place.

Those little crises help me to remember who I am. What I am. They help me switch perspectives without having to look for answers from somewhere else, say with the help of books, other people or shamanic healing remedies. When I face such a crisis moment today, I still struggle. I feel it. I look at it. I take my time to digest it with a deep knowing that the aha moment is on its way or the aha feeling. Slowly, slowly, I learned to be okay with uncomfortable thoughts, emotions and even situations without totally losing balance. It feels like I am the actor in the movie that I have created in order to learn, that I don't have to play the victim, nor the bad guy, nor the know-it-all dude. I'm just playing in the movie, co-creating a scenario that triggers the self to expand beyond believed or experienced limitations. But all these kinds of matters are very hard to put into words. Everybody has their own path. Everybody is ready when they are ready, to go to the next step, not when they read what I write. I absolutely know for myself that all the knowledge and information that I haven't learned, studied or experienced is only as valuable as my present state of consciousness. And I wholeheartedly believe that anybody who wants to know the truth and who is looking for answers won't find them by simply adding information onto the personal database or doing drugs. It is a matter of being connected, with the mind, the heart, the self or soul, the essence that makes us so unique. And in order to be there, feel it, experience it, it is not enough to study. It takes being present. And that being present seems to be one of the most difficult challenges for our Western monkey minds.

That's the reason why I practice yoga regularly. It's doesn't have to be a rigid routine. It is just a way of tuning in and connecting with your inner world and it doesn't really matter if I go for a slow walk in nature, watch the sunset, meditate, do tai chi or whatever it takes to get to that place of peace and truth inside of myself. And there I can get clarity, see things from a different perspective, take off the filtering glasses of conditioning, stop analyzing and start seeing what truly is. So in Iquitos after crossing that area of poverty, of dirt and drugs, and after overcoming the negative attack caused by a range of thoughts,

Headless Chicken

I could just let go of thoughts. And pretty instantly I was back in the here and now strolling around downtown.

I do believe that the quality of the environment you move in has an impact on the quality of thoughts and emotions, if you allow it. We are one big net of energy, like a multidimensional spider's web with individual knots or energy points. Those energy points are us. We are responsible for our energy, each and everybody. The way I vibrate has an impact on my surroundings. What is going on in my surroundings has an impact on me. If I am in the state of high awareness, I can see what's going on and respond accordingly instead of acting like a victim. Our local energy stations form the body with the help of the mind. The blueprint for that comes already with the soul. Yet, we have free will and can change anything. The challenge is to know what's best in every moment for the big spiderweb and what is your part in the big picture. So your part is just as important and just as insignificantly tiny, and yet irrecoverable and irreplaceable as mine. That is how I see it.

The spiderweb perspective calms down the monkey mind and helps to stay present. All of a sudden that day there was no more doubt, no more question, no more pondering about the future or judging the past. All that was replaced by a subtle sense of peace right where I was.

Pretty soon the last day of my three-month adventure came up. I came with a backpack and I left with a backpack, so there was nothing much to pack. The apartment was pretty clean. All I had to do was go back into town, to the smoothie place and return the keys to the shop manager before heading to the airport. But before that I went with my friend Kate from California for a goodbye drink at the market. She wanted to go to a special place that she had been introduced to by locals, where they served some kind of local hard liquor. It was fun! I hadn't been drinking other than a beer here and there. We decided to take a bottle along and go back to my place. There we met up with our joint friend the Chinese Peruvian doctor, and had a sweet last half hour to say goodbye. I gave them the rest of the food I had left and they took off together down the dirt road on that funny little motorcycle. Time to leave. I got a moto-taxi to get me to the shop, dropped off the keys and headed on directly to the airport. The Peruvian money I had was gone, just enough left to pay the taxi and get a drink at the

19 - Time to Move On

airport. Perfect.

Since I had no luggage to check in, I just strolled around the airport, got to play with some kids and talk to strangers until the counter opened to get in line for the boarding pass. By the time I got into the line there were quite some people in front of me already. So I waited and waited. I had learned to wait by now. All of a sudden I noticed some kind of general nervousness as if something had happened.

And it did: all flights were canceled with no information about when they would continue to fly. I could feel a slight adrenaline rush right into the end of my limbs after thinking: gosh, I got the ticket online, what if I don't make the connecting flight to Madrid in Lima ... I will probably lose the flight, the ticket, the connection without replacement. And what shall I do right now? I don't even have any money, no access to a bank. Plus, I just returned the keys to the apartment, and the guy is probably home by now, so I can't return there. Fuck! All those thoughts in the blink of an eye. Quickly I decided to think differently or not think at all, the latter being rather impossible. So I changed my thinking: This happens for a better outcome, I decided. Even though I don't know why and how, I accept the possibility that this disturbance can bring me a better situation with the cancellation of the flight. I just clung to that thought.

By the time it was my turn to talk to the airline personnel at the counter, it was almost midnight. Everybody else had been sent to different hotels and booked a flight the next day. So when it was my turn, most hotels and flights were booked. That's why I got a room in one of the nicest hotels close to the airport. And they managed to get me on a flight that left at a convenient time in the morning, and arrived exactly one hour before my connecting flight to Europe. So that was great. Whether it was my mindset or not that made all this happen, doesn't really matter, does it? What really matters is that I didn't give myself a hard time worrying and instead had a heck of a time in the hotel: lovely midnight dinner and moonlight swim, a great bed, nice breakfast and the connecting flight at 10 AM. Boy, I was grateful! Plus that saved me another night in some mediocre hotel in Lima, since the connecting flight was shortly after arriving. That made the trip back home really comfortable.

And that was just the beginning of a journey after the journey ...

20 - The Real Magic Starts

About Trusting versus Holding onto Habits

The end of the journey has not happened yet. I had a feeling. I also had the feeling that the work with Ayahuasca is not like taking a pill and hoping to be healed. It is merely a way to see and hear or feel clearly what is going on and what has been going on in former times. Get over the daily illusions that have been accumulating in the system during this lifetime or former lifetimes.

I have seen the limitlessness of the universe, the never-ceasing creativity. I could hear messages from some kind of higher state within myself that felt like God was talking to me. I could feel the state of bliss and awe that I was so amazed that I heard myself making sounds of admiration during ceremony. I could go back in time and be the little girl that was sexually abused. Not just remember the situation and the words, but really feel like that little girl. Therefore, I could heal and not just undertake another mental exercise. It was emotional. Emotional healing. Only by tapping into the state of being of this little girl at the time could I connect energetically with the part of myself that had been broken. Feel the pain and therefore be compassionate with that little being and allow healing to happen. I could forgive myself. That was the real secret. Forgiving myself. This is not just a mental exercise again, you feel it. It is easy to explain to yourself that a little girl of age six can't be held responsible or guilty for an adult abusing her, and therefore there is nothing to forgive to oneself. But it doesn't work like that. It is way beyond reasoning what happens energetically to a soul. I had gone back in time and relived those situations in my family life full of despair and sadness. I could feel compassion with my father and with my mother. Feel. And forgive.

20 - The Real Magic Starts

Ayahuasca gave me a glimpse into the spiritual world, nineteen times. But way before ten times, I finally knew that tripping is not the real work, nor a solution, and I still continued. The real work is to be done in the mental, emotional and physical plane in the "normal" physical world. I needed to transfer all that knowledge into every day's life now. I had to bring it all together. Going back into ceremony over and over was not the solution for me long-term. I needed to become more conscious.

How hilarious! So here we have knowledge and experiences on one side and conditioning, programs, habits on the other. And this life is not supposed to be a fight! It's about ease and grace, the state of flow, learning to ride your wave, your very own wave, while other waves from all over the place are touching you, hitting you, manipulating you. Stay centered, be yourself, not your story, a frozen imprint of the past. Fearlessly. Respond as if you had never been conditioned in the first place.

Now, I understand the full picture. I already knew before that I am not the body, I am not the emotion and I am not the thought. I am the soul. That thing with a sense of "me," that is so close to a touch of "you" without being anything touchable, I can relate to best when I'm in a trancelike state without thinking. I already knew before the trick to observe thoughts and emotions without being taken away by them. You are the observer not the thought, not the emotion. A very delicate art. If you don't manage, you may end up being taken away by a horse that went wild. Uncontrollable. It's got tremendous power. You can't control it. Doomed.

And here I am, supposed to not identify with the horse's fear and stress, while sitting right on top of it. That horse is the ego and I am the rider. I knew all that before and I used that metaphor in coaching sessions. But there is a slight difference between knowing and "feeling that knowledge" inside of you. It takes practice. Maybe some people are spontaneously enlightened and never face their ego ever again. Transcended. I doubt it. After all this journey was about not just knowing for sure, but having no more doubt. But living it in the here and now. Every day. Having it all clear. Seeing the big picture and being myself, not my story, conditioning, habit.

Headless Chicken

I couldn't just continue to live like before, with the same priorities. I looked at my life from a different viewpoint. I had already done this once before, fifteen years earlier after the cancer experience. At that time I could let go of a lot of useless fears and ideas. Things became very relative, when death knocks on the door. I could only take my kids and move to another country because I deeply felt it was right. I had no clue how I would do it. And searching for more information about work possibilities, investigating financial consequences, etc., might be important to an extent, but only to an extent. Too much planning and "making sure" is useless and distracting. Lost energy. I knew it was the right thing to do, because it felt right. Intuitively. It was very clear. And after surviving cancer, you start appreciating that kind of clarity within yourself. No need for pros and cons, no need to calculate risks and gains over and over again. "Yes but, what if … ?" the never-ending ego trying to control the process to the very detail, hoping that secures the enterprise.

And yet, fifteen years later there is a good chance to almost forget the intense lesson to surviving cancer and be influenced by the general atmosphere around you. Same with Ayahuasca. You can forget after the ceremony, once back in the habitual surroundings. And it doesn't take long to forget. That is what other guests reported as well, who had been there several times before. But you never forget for good. The truth is just a bit covered, buried somewhere deep down. You can't make the pictures unseen and the messages unheard, or all the experienced feelings disappear. But you may very possibly store that information slowly slowly away and bit by bit further away in your system. You can be distracted by your surroundings, Western life challenges, other people's opinions or loud noises of the media. Not to talk about numbing yourself with drugs, alcohol or other addictive behavior such as constantly working too much, sports, sex or social media. That's when it is so easy to become unconscious. Or keep meeting people constantly to not feel yourself. And that's exactly the point: golden glimmers and piles of shit all together in one lifetime. And now it's about transcending judgment and habit of mental and emotional autopilot toward a state of higher consciousness. It is about enabling us to choose and respond calmly with that deep knowingness of how this is all put together, trust and faith.

Two years after Ayahuasca, I still do my homework: sit, meditate, walk in the woods to enter a state of deep calmness where nothing can affect me. It's not an escape, but the opposite: looking even closer and transcending the illusion of the situation. What is really true?

Ayahuasca can't do that job for you. That's your own work. Become clear. Become aware of what really is and how you can create that reality. And finally, let go, let God in and trust. Stop trying to prevent a lion killing you that was never there in the first place. Stop trying to control and to manipulate your surroundings, but become a master of your mind, the rider and friend of that horse. Make peace with all sides of yourself. Love yourself completely, including the uneven parts. That's the work! And that Ayahuasca won't do for you. It opens that door so you can have a glimpse, but you still have to walk through, day by day. At least, it didn't do it for me or anybody I know. Speaking about what you've seen, heard, felt and experienced is one thing. But how you respond in daily life is another.

That's why I believe it's absolutely necessary to have some kind of a practice to stay connected with that innermost part of yourself. Some people just look at the sea, or breathe consciously. Others read the Bible and pray or practice yoga. Some can maintain that elevated state of consciousness in every moment. They never disconnect. For me a little daily practice and a somewhat healthier, balanced lifestyle helps me to stay connected with my essence and keep the "tubes" clean. This way I am not overwhelmed by the monkey mind's chatter, hormonal imbalances and the wide range of feelings a human experiences.

Experiencing without judging, that's the art. Choosing how to respond, that's the freedom. Clarity of mind and focus that's how you create. Feelings fuel the process and create momentum, mobilize energy. Sounds so easy ...

* * *

Coming back to the "real world" was quite interesting: I had no plan what to do next. And after all this tripping it was quite easy for a while to let go of compulsive thinking, pondering and planning without freaking out. So I was just open and responsive to what life would bring up. I knew I would go back to Mallorca. I knew I love to help people expand their box, or even free themselves, feel better. I knew that is my own path, too, continue to expand. I love coaching in this rather fun way I had been doing it, outdoors while walking. I enjoy modeling and improv and I really like film acting. That is already quite something. Then there is still more to discover. Exciting.

On the way back from Lima to Palma I had planned to stop over in Madrid for a few days to meet my old friend from university. We had a heck of a time. In the evening, I faced my first little challenge: we would go out with another friend we had known for a long time. And with that girl's newish "secret lover," an oldish chap, married, charming, rich and bored. I could perfectly relate to him having a great time taking that twenty-five-year-younger chick out. I could also perfectly relate to her, being admired, receiving gifts and escaping a life that had become nothing but habit, also her emotional and sexual life. Here I am, an external observer grateful to be free of judgment and yet honest. So I told her what I saw and felt without blame or interpreting much into the story. I didn't feel compelled to get involved anyway. This is not my problem. But, yes, I shared my truth. After a few days I left for Mallorca. A few months later my friend told me, our friend had finished the secret affair and took it as a learning experience. Today she is happier and also still with her husband. She now knows what she really wants and dares to express herself.

Arriving in Mallorca felt weird. My apartment felt so sterile after all those luscious green surroundings during those three months. Soon, I picked up my daily morning routine down by the beach again. I kept myself calm, with no clue where the next lot of money was coming from.

After a few weeks a friend of mine called me to come to Malaga. I had studied there and I liked the place. It wouldn't be much of a deal. I had time. And I fancied going down there just to hang out with some friends. The only concern was: can I afford another trip? And it was less about whether I have the money, but about if it was okay to continue traveling without ever working. Or will I get a horrible wake-up call some day? It was interesting to observe this programmed fear. Nothing more to it. So I checked prices, got a great deal on a return ticket for 50 bucks and took off for five days. No big deal. Just a nice time living life. Enjoying.

On the way back I missed my plane by five minutes. I had wanted to leave for the airport half an hour earlier, but my friend said we would have enough time to get there by leaving a little bit later. Well, we

20 - The Real Magic Starts

didn't. I arrived eight minutes past boarding time at the airport. By the time I reached the gate, the plane had left five minutes earlier. Shit happens!

In the meantime my friend had gone to work. I realized a nervousness coming up. Did I fuck it up? I didn't blame my friend, because it was still my decision when to leave. I had agreed with his idea. I had never liked to blame others for my decisions. So I went to the various counters to check for an alternative flight. Obviously, I had to buy a new ticket. They wanted 400 bucks. That was way beyond OK with me, and more than I was willing to spend even if I had to travel via Frankfurt. I did have a financial cushion, but I didn't want to go to the edge. So I kept looking and found another ticket late at night. Done. Problem solved. Another potential mini-drama story over.

I took the train into the center of town. Hung out and strolled around the areas I remembered when I was studying there, twenty years ago. I strolled through the market, passed by the house that I rented at the time. A huge flat that I subleased to four roommates, all guys from different countries. Together we would pass by the market almost every day to get fresh fruit. Then we would go home loaded with kilos of vitamins, and live mostly off milkshakes. What a great time we had! Eventually, we would organize parties spontaneously. Everybody could invite anybody. And so we did. The shack was perfect for partying. Huge, old, a hair dresser underneath that was closed at night ...

There in Malaga, this sensation of synchronized moments came up as if there was some kind of a plan behind that day: it felt like I was drawn from one place to another and was always at the right place at the right time. Funny enough that only happened after missing the plane. I bumped into interesting people, interesting shops, interesting situations. Nothing super important, but very interesting. I felt like I was part of one big play, where everybody is part of the orchestra, and one superior force is directing and putting it altogether, so it fits, synchronized.

Shortly after arriving at home, I had the next invitation: the Canadian lady I had known the year before during a meeting and whom I had met for coffee once or twice afterwards, had contacted me. We had made friends. She was in London right now and that was the perfect moment to meet up again, she thought.

Headless Chicken

London is a great place, and I would have loved to have met her, but that was really beyond my budget right now, considering hotel and dining on the street. She understood. We agreed on meeting next time she came to the island.

A lot of friends came to see me after they found out I had come back from the jungle. I could tell some of them were hoping to find a mega guru to tell them about healing powers of natural shamanic hallucinogens. It did not happen. All I could tell them was that I don't believe you should trust anybody's personal experiences neither with Ayahuasca nor follow anybody's opinion unless you feel it in the guts. I did share my experiences briefly. Especially the fact that the past had not been removed, but I could see it clearly now, feel it, become compassionate with myself, forgive myself and let go. Also that out of all the experiences I had, beautiful as well as ugly visions, messages, physical pains and very weird stuff, nothing was brand new to me. It was more like a confirmation of something I already knew, but not remembered and doubted.

Also, that for me, the work is not over by doing Ayahuasca, the real work is in the real life, when it comes to being present, being yourself, not your story, not your program. One girl who had experienced sexual abuse in childhood from a family member really thought she could take the drug and the past would change or just disappear. What about what you learned from the experience? Compassion? Forgiveness? Love? Wiping it away is not much of a help, in order not to run into abusive situations in the future or to become the abuser yourself. The psyche already does it unconsciously when you are little, in order to protect and survive these moments, when you just couldn't cope with the situation: just wipe it out, forget it. But then, when it shows up again, that's an invitation to go there and heal it. At least, that's what I believe.

Using any kind of recreational drugs is a mere intent to make you feel better in the moment, or not having to feel what is truly there, something that is there and that is uncomfortable. Using a drug is like covering the uncomfortable feeling, and the wounds can never really heal underneath. Ayahuasca doesn't do that: first of all, it's not comfortable, it is physically very uncomfortable; it can be very scary and distressing. It can only give a glimpse into the truth, as much as you can take in the moment, as much as is good for you in

20 - The Real Magic Starts

this moment of this lifetime. Nothing more. It doesn't last. The past doesn't go away, but you can make peace with it and stop suffering by understanding, being compassionate and forgiving.

* * *

It was springtime in Mallorca, just beautiful: the quality of the light, the clear skies, nature about to explode, great energy. I decided to enjoy and not think too much, especially not to worry. And the decision seemed to be good enough for it to work.

My Canadian friend sent me another email, telling me she had spontaneously changed plans and booked an Airbnb flat in Paris with an extra room waiting for me to join her. All it took was another ticket and since we had a flat, I wouldn't need much budget on food on the street. Okay, you really could go over there I figured. And I sure looked forward to seeing her. I might as well use the visit to Paris to find some agencies to represent me as a model at the same time. Get some modeling work and fill up the account. Next thing you know, I got a reasonable ticket in the following week and a couple of appointments with model agencies. Cool! Decision taken. Feels right. Let go of planning and stay tuned.

* * *

On a sunny afternoon before leaving for Paris, I was sitting on my terrace with a beautiful view of the ocean. Springtime is just lovely. That woman I had met just recently called me. She was my age and we connected instantly. And she was very engaged in her spiritual development, searching for ways to find out how to live up to her life purpose. She believed in shamanic work, did workshops and seminars, read books, saw videos and was very open for any kind of information that would support that goal. She seemed to work hard on that.

She told me little bit about her story when she called and I could hear in her voice that she would appreciate someone to share with. So I invited her spontaneously to come over for tea. Shortly after, we were both enjoying the beautiful sea-view. Anne had finally gotten over a long-term relationship that she felt had led her nowhere. She wanted to have kids; he didn't want to have any more kids, since he already had kids. She had become like a life manager and something had gone out of balance in the relationship. They separated because they decided they didn't have the same outlook on life. But he was still very attached to her. And finally after years, he let go of her and moved on. She felt released at first and free and at the same time doubt crossed her mind: would it be possible at all to find that perfect match, that twin soul that she had wished for on this island? It was true, Mallorca was an interesting place when it comes to relationships. Many people come here and separate. And many people live here and never settle in the relationship. It's a touristic place, sun, beach, fun. As soon as a problem appears, people seem to take it not as a chance to evolve, but as an exit to not get any deeper.

Hearing her concerns made me laugh. I remember sitting down in my chair leaning back and talking to her very convinced of what I was saying. I said, "Of course you will find the right guy or he will find you. It's not about the place. It's about you. When you are ready he will show up faster than you can imagine." At that point I still thought I was talking to her, which very shortly turned out to be my own destiny ...

* * *

After a couple of hours talking she left and I packed my bag because the following day I would take off to Paris. The next day I decided to take the car into town, park and take the airport bus, which was quite convenient.

In the meantime, the French girlfriend of a dear hippie friend of mine had contacted me by email. She was in her seventies and lived in Paris. I told her that I was coming and she suggested to meet up upon my arrival, which I found very sweet.

So I arrived at the low-cost airport out of Paris, took the bus downtown and that's where she was waiting for me. How sweet! I was really touched. I had only met her briefly before in Mallorca. We had a lovely time in one of those typical dark French coffee shops. She was so French! A former lawyer and mother, a well-rounded, clear and interesting person. It was a lot of fun to share our stories and what we cared about. Different. Yes, just really sweet.

20 - The Real Magic Starts

After a couple of hours I took the Metro and headed for the apartment that my friend had rented. It took me about an hour to get there. I forgot which arrondissement it was, but it was a pleasant area, a bit off the beaten track, with a Parisian charm, conveniently connected to public transportation.

The flat was on the fourth floor without an elevator. For me I like to travel with just a backpack, not a problem at all. I rang the bell and there she was: Betty! A real world citizen. A lady in her early seventies who spends her lifetime mostly traveling all over the world since her retirement. I had hardly spent any time with her before and just felt like we knew each other from another time. We had some kind of connection, confidence and trust. It is interesting to observe how life brings people together. No matter what age, no matter what nationality, no matter what background. Betty and I had very interesting honest conversations. We talked about private issues as well as topics that both concerned us:

Where are we going from here? What is the right thing to do? How to deal with difficult situations and complicated family relationships. What had we learned so far? What were our biggest fears and dreams? Betty used to be a hard-core businesswoman, highly successful, experienced and well connected. And yet, when it came down to what's truly important to us in life, we shared the same values. Even though I had been running a publishing company for ten years and organizing seminars all over the world, I never felt like a businesswoman. Yet a little hard core. We both felt, it all comes down to love, connection, relationships. No money in the world can buy you that kind of freedom that makes you feel rounded and at peace, comfortable. Obviously, we live in a world where money has become the one and only way of making a living. No money, no house, no food, no tomorrow, it seems. On the other hand, very few people starve from hunger in our society. Everything is relative. Therefore, we need to question what we think, our beliefs, our thoughts, what we feel. We need to learn to distinguish between what is really true and what is our personal interpretation, faded by psychological and emotional conditioning from the past. We need to be clear, find a way to give the thinking mind a break in order to see the bigger picture. We need to dare to share, open up fearlessly in order to connect and contribute to something bigger than ourselves. Betty had a very turbulent and exciting life. She gave me her biography as a gift. I started reading while being in Paris at night.

Headless Chicken

The book confirmed that we can trust no matter how astonishing or unbelievable or scary the situation, there is a variety of possible outcomes, sometimes much more exciting than we can even imagine.

What made us first connect, Betty and I, was her project of a new way of living for "aging" people, or retired people, people who don't spend their days going to work and don't live in a typical family situation. I had no pension plan, nor regular income, and the question of how to live later on crossed my mind from time to time. I felt it would be cool to share your knowledge, love and potential with younger people in a simple, unsophisticated and free way. The traditional idea of family life where grandparents take care of their grandchildren and kids take over the parents' business seemed very outdated. I would rather imagine some kind of co-living with friends, new friends and maybe family, if they are interested in bringing their talents into that potential project.

My vision for Betty's project was a more open one. I had a whole load of ideas of how I visualized to live later on in life. I saw a think tank, a therapeutic network, people who've become friends of all ages. People who care, people who were willing to share, people who are more interested in the benefit of all than in just a personal interest. All this without this being a hippie community. I don't really know about hippie communities, just that the word can have a negative touch to it, as if people wanted to hang out all day smoking pot, having wild sex and praying to the sun, ha ha …

The week passed very quickly. We did a little sightseeing, culture and coffee-shopping together. A few times I cooked and we had a cozy evening at home. We also spent time alone, doing our own thing, so I visited a couple of model agencies and got contracted by a major one. I remember seeing the Parisians smiling even less than the Germans and the Spanish.

Street musicians in the subways gave a relieving break from the gray cold ambience of the famous world city. I really don't know why they call it the city of love.

There were quite young people working in the bakery shop on the corner of the street next to the Metro station. I went there every day to get a croissant. Every day, no matter what time of day, these young

20 - The Real Magic Starts

people looked seriously unhappy, unmotivated. It was shocking to me. No smile ever. As a hopeless optimist, who kind of cares even for strangers, I talked to them to find out about their day. Obviously, there was not much time to get involved into a serious conversation when you're working behind a bakery counter, but boy, I wish I would have made a difference by asking them to look a little beyond the habitual thinking and question how to make a difference in the here and now. How to stop suffering from unease and discontentment. The typical helper syndrome. So I kept quiet.

And soon I found myself sitting in the plane heading back to Mallorca. I was reflecting on my experiences in Paris, the conversations I had with Betty and what was going on in her life. I was reflecting on the people who never take a break to feel and listen inside and become responsible and compassionate. I was reflecting on my life. How we get lost in some kind of hypnotic trance state in every day's life without noticing. How we get trapped in expectations of society. How we still have programs of fear running, even though we are aware of that fact. How we allow to be totally manipulated, as if we have become nothing, but a product of the system.

I found myself in a situation where I felt like it doesn't really matter whether I go right or left, if I became a hip middle-aged actress, acting in inspiring movies or settled down in the middle of nowhere growing potatoes. Nothing seemed to matter, really, other than the chance of living that very moment consciously. And that went on for quite some time, until the thinking brain kicked in, running the old program of what I had been told about how you should live your life. Set a goal, plan the steps and keep track of reaching step-by-step.

But now, after my "spiritual confirmation," that way of living had become ridiculously limiting. Why should I limit myself to one idea? Plus, there is a good chance that those so-called goals are nothing more than implants of others. Obviously, that approach to life can make you also very stuck, without doing anything at all, due to the inability to choose from all those possibilities. Or feel very floaty as you pursue those steps and feel you are not getting anywhere, disconnected. But when including something else into the equation, that something else that is beyond the thinking mind, call it gut feeling, intuition, sixth sense, then, the whole approach became an exciting journey, as if you really could see the world, like you had never seen it before.

Headless Chicken

You open your eyes in the morning, and the habitual chatter in your mind is turned off. Never kicked in. And you see this very morning for the very first time. Feels like freedom. The monkey mind easy peasy, the body relaxed, a state of ease and grace. Wow! That's what I really want!

After all these Ayahuasca ceremonies and insights, that state only lasts as long as I stay conscious. Ayahuasca doesn't do the job. And this ability to stay conscious takes a certain intention, decision, consistency, faith. For me, what I've learned is to notice immediately when the ego mind is interfering in order to take control of the process. It's quite easy to detect, become aware of, because it is almost always uncomfortable. So once I'm aware, I can look deeper and see what's real and what's habitual autopilot running. And if I manage to not take this so serious, I don't have to give myself a hard time. I can smile, despite whatever program is trying to take me over. I can be at ease, despite whatever I experience. Take it, dare to feel it, leave it.

I love to meditate in a plane. I guess I have conditioned myself to do so since I have been traveling so many times over the ocean and many of those long-distance travels with small children. That gave me a chance to train to get in a trancelike state while still being totally conscious of what is going on and at the same time to become patient. Well, the patience part I am still working on.

One more time that year I arrive at the airport of Palma de Mallorca. It was only April, not even one month after leaving the jungle. The temperature was already pleasant. Winter in Mallorca can be very uncomfortable. Temperatures below 10 Celsius with high humidity. That was another reason for me to dare to take off for the jungle experience so spontaneously.

I took the bus from the airport into Palma to get my car and decided to get some groceries on the way back home to finally fill up the fridge.

The supermarket at Joan Miro came into my mind. Not that I particularly liked it, it just appeared and I wasn't too far from it, so I went there. As I entered the store a thought crossed my mind: I bet I see somebody I know … You know that feeling when you are, e.g., at the airport and think to yourself, I wonder who I will bump into today? Maybe I am just more attentive than others. Well, this happens

20 - The Real Magic Starts

to me quite a bit and is nothing spectacular. Mallorca isn't that big anyway. I go in, pass the cashier and there he stands in the middle of the fruit and vegetable section: my former aikido teacher!

I had seen him only once in class. I had been looking for an alternative to a fighting martial art after the one-month kung fu experience. Kung fu training was great, but fighting, I just don't do. Aikido was right. Peaceful. As much as I loved aikido and his class at the time, I never returned. That was a year ago. Now that I saw him again, I wondered why I never went back. And I saw it clearly: he couldn't be my aikido teacher. Why? It didn't matter. It just was like that and I knew.

We talked for ten or fifteen minutes, which is quite a long time for standing in the fruit section of a busy supermarket. We exchanged numbers and decided to meet up sometime soon to talk about our joint interests: coaching, spirituality, how to support people who need help, our own experiences. I felt something big. Call it epic energy moving. But it wasn't like a romantic hormonal trip. It was different. All I knew was that this story was already written. I didn't have to worry about whether this was going to become a love story, a business relationship, or another form of friendship. It didn't matter. No need to figure out a label to what this might become. No box needed. This story had been already written, and I could lean back and enjoy the ride. Fearlessly.

A couple days later Anthony called me. I was really excited to meet him later at my place. Funny enough, I didn't want to invite any man I didn't know too well anymore into my flat. Being an open and somewhat kind woman, I had run into tight situations in my own flat, where a guy interpreted my invitation for coffee as invitation for more, which left me kind of shocked. But this time with Anthony, there was no way that he would be like that. And I did want to meet him at home and not in a coffeeshop. So I did, without fear of running into an uncomfortable situation.

The bell rings and there he is: dressed in tight jeans, boots and a leather jacket. Oh yes, he's black, or brown, I didn't really notice it before. We sat at the kitchen table, drank tea and talked and talked and talked. We shared experiences, what we cared about, what was important for us in life, what we had learned so far, and what we wanted to contribute to the world. It seems like a blink of an eye and seven hours were gone.

The same happened a few days later. Seven hours. And a few days later. That day, I had people working in my place to repair a water damage. They were drilling and knocking out part of the wall, but nothing would bother us. Still, we both felt comfortable, trusting that it was absolutely safe to be vulnerable. It felt like we knew each other from before. And suddenly I did remember: that's the guy I saw in a ceremony! The day shaman Francisco sang for me to heal my childhood trauma. When I cried out loud for ages. When I felt broken, lost and devastated, absolutely hopeless that there would be a single way of living life without feeling guilty about my self, ever. And then, I could forgive myself, and rose like a queen sitting on the throne, occupying my own place in my own life. And after that, that Buddha-like guy appeared across from me the queen, and we sat across from each other for ages while drifting upward an endless spiral into eternity. That was the picture I saw. And that was him, Anthony.

No reason to freak out, no reason to interpret, dream, wish, visualize, project anything on him. He was just some kind of a twin soul or something. No matter what that meant and no matter what consequences that might have.

He shared his stuff, and I shared mine. Fearlessly. Honestly. It felt good.

I didn't worry, I didn't think too much, I just was. Like that queen sitting on her throne being okay with whatever there is.

* * *

During that time an old friend that I hadn't seen in ten years contacted me asking how I was. So I told him I had just come back from the jungle and I had let go of doubt. He knew me very well. We were dating during sometime and had worked together on a few projects. He was a philanthropist and so was I. We worked on humanitarian projects together. Turns out he had moved to Valencia from France and had his home base and office there now. He still traveled a lot but right now happened to be in Valencia for a few weeks. So he spontaneously asked me to come over for a visit to catch up. We have been in contact during all those years every once in awhile, but never visited each other. It seemed like now would be a good time. Again, I really couldn't worry too much about whether I could afford to spend the money for another

20 - The Real Magic Starts

airline ticket because it was ridiculously inexpensive. What the heck! I just booked the tickets.

It was a very early flight, so I decided to sleep in Palma at a friend's house, where I had shared a flat before. That would make the trip to the airport very quick and convenient, that early in the day. Also, I looked up a few agencies again to combine the trip with visiting model agencies again and made a few appointments. I only went for a long weekend.

Before I left, I met Anthony again. One more time, he came to my place for the third or fourth time. I had already packed. Again, six hours passed quickly. We decided to go into town and have a drink. I would sleep in Santa Catalina, so we chose the bar in the hood.

We could just sit and talk forever. Nothing had happened, physically. But everything else had already happened: we were deeply connected. We already had a relationship. Something deeper than what we had experienced before, either of us. After midnight, Anthony brought me to my place so I could get some rest before traveling.

When saying goodbye downstairs at the door, we both felt this attraction. We both felt something. It was okay. No problem, no urge, no hurry, no fear, no need to talk, just a deep sensation and a longing. We just kissed on the cheek, shared a warm long hug and said goodbye. When he left, we both turned around and looked into each other's eyes, knowing that this story was already written. No need to control, worry, plan.

I love to get up early in the morning to go to the airport to fly somewhere. Especially if I can travel light with a backpack only. Off I go. It was six thirty in the morning when I caught the bus. The bus came every twenty minutes this time of day and I just about made it. Traveling with low-cost airlines you have to be really careful to not spend more money than regular tickets would cost. My backpack was just about still considered hand luggage and I could take it on board. I had my boarding pass printed already, so I could go right away to the gate. Easy and smooth.

Not even an hour later I arrived in Valencia. My friend Sam was waiting for me at the gate. It felt like yesterday that we last met. Still the same gentleman. Opening the door for me to enter the car. We went and had a coffee in Valencia city, strolled around a bit, visited the fair grounds and sites and had a great time catching up. Our work, the children, the personal life. We both were still the same: high standards of ethics when it comes to mission and work. That's what bonded us. I took advantage and stopped by a model agency that I had contacted, to leave my material. I had a funky feeling about this agency. They didn't seem to be very professional. Well, I thought to myself, Valencia is kind of a big village, don't expect so much. So I decided not to visit the other agencies. I just sent them my portfolio by email. After that, we started heading to his home. He lived an hour's drive south of Valencia in a little coastal village very close, by the sea in a nice new three-bedroom apartment.

When a woman visits a man or vice versa and they have been dating before and now are both single, it's good to make clear what you want. At least for me it's like that. In my personal history I often had not been able to say no, since I was a kid. It is very important to me today to make things clear. No false expectations or anything. I asked where I can sleep. He said, I could sleep anywhere I wanted. So I asked to sleep in the master bedroom upstairs, and if he was kind enough to sleep downstairs, in the living area level in one of the kid's bedroom. Clear. Good!

It was interesting to see how well we got along with each other, still. We went across the street to the supermarket, bought some basics and cooked together. Then we kept on talking and talking and talking and finally went to bed. Well, I did. He is a night worker, sitting on the computer writing concepts and projects all night long to almost morning.

The next day we went for long stroll on the seaside and visited the center of the coastal village. Walking and talking for hours. I also told him about my Ayahuasca experiences. Even though he's the last person I could think of doing shamanic healing ceremonies. But I knew he would understand. And he did.

In the evening we went to have Asian food and watched the movie *Lucy* that night. Sitting in the living room across from Sam watching the movie, I had a lot of intense positive, upbeat feelings and sensations going on inside of me. I was much more aware of everything that

20 - The Real Magic Starts

was going on inside and outside of me than before Peru. Just like in the movie *Lucy*, she becomes more and more aware of everything, everywhere and accesses any information.

Gosh, what's going on? I felt sensations of sexual arousal! Out of the blue. Something must be really wrong here. I'm sitting in the wrong living room. I don't want anything from my friend Sam, at least not that. Well, that was clear, and I made it clear. I just hoped he did not pick up on my feelings and misinterpret. He was a very sensitive guy. Looking deeper I realized that those sensations stemmed from thoughts and memories of the time spent with Anthony. Much more than a hundred miles away, I finally allowed myself to feel. Interesting! It was safe to feel whatever was there. No confrontation. And Sam was a person of confidence, a guy I could trust to share what was going on inside of me with. So I did. I wanted him to know. Even though nothing had happened with Anthony so far, Sam was happy for me.

Time went flying and soon we headed back to the airport. I couldn't wait to get back to see Anthony and tell him the truth. I really didn't care whether he was feeling the same or not. I was absolutely okay with becoming totally vulnerable, as long as I had the guts to be truthful to myself. No role, no mask, no stories, just being myself. Honest, truthful, naked.

We had planned on seeing each other on Tuesday, but when I headed to the airport on Monday, I sent him a text telling him I would be there around noontime. I considered asking him if he wanted to meet up that very same day. But he had already sent a text back, suggesting to meet up right away, when I arrived and picked up my car in town. Great! I couldn't wait any longer!

I had parked around Plaza Progreso and he was supposed to be waiting in the bar there. When I crossed the light toward the bar with my backpack, he came out of the bar and walked toward me. I felt happy! Not really excited, rather relieved. We hugged dearly. He kissed my neck smoothly. Which was an accident, as he said later.

That was it. Ever since, we were a couple. We kept on talking a lot. We both needed a lot of time alone, to meditate or listen inside. We both liked practicing regularly and maintaining some sacred rituals. Chi kung, aikido, tai chi, yoga or just sitting by the sea, going for a swim in the ocean. We both liked a simple life. Shibumi, the elegance of simplicity.

Shortly after, a friend of mine asked me if I would take care of the dog of his friends and live in his apartment for a couple of months. It was just before I was going to move back into my friend's house in Santa Catalina and Anthony had to leave the place he stayed as well. So that's when Anthony and I pretty spontaneously moved together. In the meantime we moved several times. We had difficult times, questions, ideas, dreams, ups and downs just like anybody else, but not really: we don't project our shit on the other person. We take the time and effort to look inside regularly, not only when things become tense, tight or uncomfortable. We dare to share. And we still get stuck. Show ourselves with all facets of black, white, limitless shades of gray and the colorful rays in between. We both know everything has an end to it and then a new beginning comes, yes or yes.

21 - What Difference Did the Shamanic Work Make?

Years after Ayahuasca

The most important difference of the three-month experience in the Peruvian Amazon and nineteen Ayahuasca ceremonies is how I experience life today. But I sincerely believe, it was not the Ayahuasca that taught me anything, but me opening up to the bigger field, the one, God. I still forget and I still get stuck and I still have ego. I see clearer today. I see my part in it. I still make errors. And I have faith that I can be forgiven, if I ask for it. And I can forgive myself.

Life is a constant change and I am okay to go along with it. Perception of reality has changed. It not only looks like but feels like life is a journey of the soul that is written, directed, and played by me. Limitless scenarios and possibilities with the same intention: This here is my chance to heal, experience, expand, have fun, exchange, create and mostly love.

I know I am an individual and I know that I am part of the whole big mass, connected. I am you and you are me and we tend to project and interpret and create stuff that is in our minds onto the screen that our physical eyes can see, our physical body can experience and our feelings can sense, a so-called life experience.

The big question always was: who is me? Only when I understand that can I really be free and live what I came here for. And this knowing what I came here for is nothing that can be answered in the thinking mind. That knowingness is located somewhere deeper. There is this part of the mind that can witness, think, draw conclusions. Then there is another part which is accessible only in a certain way, not by thinking. Psychologists might call that part of the unconscious. That part is connected with everything. As if there was one big database, one big

Headless Chicken

mass of energy and I have access to it, once I find out how. Since I am also part of that very mass of energy, I am directly connected and influenced by everything. I also influence everything, consciously or unconsciously. I don't need to know how. I do it anyway, whether I am aware of it or not: I suck in information in the form of energy qualities and I project information in form of energy qualities. I shine out the color of the light I vibrate in. If I am unaware, everything happens unconsciously and I am a mere tourist who takes an organized trip, preplanned by others, just like thousands and thousands of others who are doing the same. It's organized so it seems to be kind of comfortable. The only drag is, we don't get to create the journey ourselves, choose the details, find out which path is ours to walk, according to our uniqueness. The tour operator has managed to sell us his trips in the most profitable way and we buy it blindly, deaf and numb like the three monkeys. Unconsciously consuming like hell, highly manipulated, caught in fear and escapism.

For some people there is some healing to do. For others some learning. For others some sharing. I assume we all have a little bit of everything to do. The clue is to figure out how to switch from tourist to traveler, from pre-organized to self-determined and self-fulfilling. To let go and trust God directly instead of the tour operator and the travel insurance.

Ayahuasca can give us only glimpses into what we need to see beyond the known of the conscious mind, when we need it, in order to heal, learn, or just grow.

It can be very uncomfortable and scary, physically, emotionally and mentally. And, it is a little bit like a pill that you take. It serves you in your present moment, maybe to get over childhood trauma, depression or other addictive patterns. In that sense, it can free you. But then you need to make this your own. Yes, what you have seen once cannot be made unseen. What you have felt once, cannot be made unfelt. What you have experienced, cannot be wiped out. However, it can be forgotten. Covered over by the dust of everyday habitual life, because we allow our attention and energy to go everywhere else than where we most need it, within ourselves. Our decisions are no longer our decisions. We are manipulated, without knowing, become victims of technology instead of masters, spending half our lifetime to tell Facebook what we like and what not, and how we are best manipulated. And we are

21 - What Difference Did the Shamanic Work Make?

all so used to manipulating others. And we willingly go along, because we are not attentive, we get trapped in induced fears. Lions that never appear. And no matter how much Ayahuasca and meditation, the ego is not dead and can still keep you in check without you realizing. At least that is my personal observation.

※ ※ ※

From all the people I have talked to, who visited the retreat center in those three months, there was none of those who had been coming back once or several times who did not mention that life would not become easier after Ayahuasca. In fact, most of them said they would come back to do another ceremony or several, to reconnect with that knowledge, to remember, to bring it back to the surface. And that's exactly my point: no matter what kind of practice, ceremonies or healing you do, it is not the pill for a happy ending. Simply because there is no ending, this story never ends, the story that you write, experience, are. It is a process, not a destination. One day, we will leave the body, but our energy moves on. Nonbelievers, atheists and critics may stick this truth into Einstein's theories: Energy cannot be killed, it can only be transformed. I'm not a total fan of science. I love mathematics, the triangle, how it all evens out and adds up, and chemistry and physics, wow! It is so cool to find out how things work, the intelligence behind. And the more you know, the more you realize how little you know and especially how everything is so relative. The latest scientific research receives prize awards today and ten years later can seem ridiculously misleading according to the state-of-the-art scientific knowledge by then. I believe there is one God behind all this universe and we just try to figure out how the magic works with science. The magic was already there, when we found out.

It comes down to being present in every moment. But what does that really mean? To me, it means being in a state of peace. Safe. Rather a witness of thoughts, mental chatter, mechanisms, that work all automatized, habits, conditionings, patterns, words, expressions, interpretations, desires, likes and dislikes, compulsive reactions and last of all feelings and emotions, than identifying with them. Being present in the here and now without getting totally overwhelmed by what is going on around me.

Headless Chicken

Feelings are a big lesson for me, a difficult one, because where I grew up, it was preferable to learn to shut up and behave instead of allowing to feel or even express what you feel. It is as if I had to learn how to feel, or learn how to not hide that feeling, and especially to dare to share it, like learning a new discipline or sport. And I bet the generations before me had the same issue.

When I am aware, I can witness. I can be myself not identify with programs and ego, even those are still there. Only then can I be myself, not my story, not what I have been taught, but live what I truly feel is right. Only then can I be responsible for my life, knowing now that I am. Only then can I relate to others, not just be the mask, a role, or clone of my parents or the direct opposite of them.

As much as Ayahuasca can open doors, we still have to walk through the door over and over again, step-by-step throughout the whole life, that is my perspective as of today. And that's the whole idea: We didn't come here to jump to a happy ending and never move again. It is about the path, not just reaching a goal. Otherwise you would take a helicopter to get to the top of the Himalayas and check that box.

One big thing that I learnt the very first night was an isight about duality, as I described in the first chapters. Why it exists. How to deal with it. How to let go of suffering. The others did not receive that insight. Everybody has to walk their own path and when they are ready for the next step, the next stepping stone shows up. It is more a matter of faith than searching in Ayahuasca for the next lesson. The lesson shows up anyway. And then, you have to make it part of yourself, don't bury it under the big carpet, where all of the things you didn't like are "forgotten," hidden and stored. Not getting the lesson, we just recreate different situations with the same lesson until we get it.

In the two years after coming back from Peru a lot of things have happened. Some of them I shared, such as bumping into Anthony in the supermarket and recognizing him.

That could have happened just the same without my Peruvian experiences.

21 - What Difference Did the Shamanic Work Make?

I do not try to evaluate, judge, plan, wish for, manipulate a situation anyway, now more conscious about it. It still happens, but then I let go. I just let it be, let it evolve.
This state of allowing is a very delicate flower that needs to be taken care of. It takes some kind of conscious tender loving care, a discipline, a hygiene. Also I know I haven't learned anything really. I just learned how to learn, now I have got to do the job, day by day.

Soon after getting together with Anthony, I had received a phone call from a modeling agency in Valencia, one that I had not even visited during my stay a few weeks earlier. They booked me without a casting for a ten-day cruise trip from Norway to Russia and back. This was my first income in ages. And it was quite fun cruising the Northern Sea, being made-up, all included.

That's how life keeps showing and teaching me, that it's okay to let go. Set your compass, just feel and let go. That's why it's so important to be connected to the inner world. Because this is where the compass is. You still have to set it. That is the difficult part. Otherwise, it's going to follow a route that you accidentally set, unconsciously. Maybe out of fear in order to prevent damage. Fear of the lion that never shows up.

* * *

I realized that the wishes and dreams that come up in the mind can be very insignificant. Just pure mind fuck. What really matters is, when you feel sensations of anything similar to love. That is other than a hype.

I described it like that, because love is hard to describe in words. For me, it is the sensation of peace, subtle joy, unity with everything there is, compassion. It's not a hype or ecstasy, but again, everybody has to find out for themselves, what their basic most important value is for them. That which is most important, more important than anything else. Those people who have suffered life-threatening diseases and survived know that surviving is more important than driving your dream car. Those people who haven't been able to pay the rent or even don't have sufficient food know that behind that existential fear is still something else: connection. A Nelson Mandela in prison, a Gandhi in India, a Martin Luther King or a Jesus have related to and talked about

Headless Chicken

that something else. It is up to us to make that connection, and it's not an external thing, it doesn't come from Ayahuasca, it's a process inside of us. A pill won't do. It's a knowingness and a feeling of a higher intelligence working through us that wants to be heard and consciously chosen a life long. The way we do the things we do is how we create. Not just what we decide to do. It's about the quality of our thoughts, the quality of the words we use, and how we respond to situations in our daily life. For me it is like this: we come with all the information already available in us. All I have to do is set an intention, get out of the way and allow it to happen. This getting out of the way is the most difficult part. In somewhat common language one would refer to transcending ego, I suppose. Instead of being mad at parts of ourselves or others that possibly stem from our ancestors and that have been stored in the subconscious, stuff that seems to sabotage our forthcoming, we start becoming compassionate and forgiving.

Feeling bad about yourself or never feeling good enough or simply never even questioning what you really are about results in lack. Missing something that nothing and nobody can give us, unless we allow to open up for it inside. Instead of fighting with parts of ourselves we don't like, we can acknowledge, appreciate and be okay with them. And by doing so, we free ourselves from what feels like the devil within us. Then we can transform the bullshit and feel the love that we are. But that process takes a whole lot of consciousness. That's the work. That's the real medicine. That's where the power is. And where the freedom is.

What else has changed in those last years is my attitude toward work. Throughout life I had a strange relationship with money. When my father committed suicide, the story I was told was he had worked too hard and had money problems. So I grew up under the impression that money and work can be life threatening.

I always had more than I needed. During my studies of business administration I did weekend jobs and worked at fairs. I had a half-orphan's pension from the state of Germany that already paid for my room. I always had more than I needed.

Today, I don't work regularly. And it's still the same: I always have more than I need. I had worked in a "proper" business, ran a publishing company, burnt out, felt low, depressed, guilty of spending very little

21 - What Difference Did the Shamanic Work Make?

time with my young children. I couldn't sleep well at night during many years and had eating disorders. We had a nice home, nice cars, reputation, stayed in five-star hotels all over the place. Multitasking, smiling, looking good, jiggling tasks and losing contact to the love inside.

Obviously, you can't relate to others if you don't relate to yourself first. So the relationship broke due to two people who were not in touch with themselves, just functioning really well in the material world. Leaving the money behind was the easier part of separating. When I invented that new job as a half-day walking coach, I earned exactly the money that I needed to live as a single mom with two children downtown Munich. My beliefs determined the outcome of my life. It was obvious.

* * *

Today, I enjoy small incidents just as much as a business deal. Meeting someone on the street who needs an ear to listen to him or her. It's amazing how situations appear almost like pearls of the necklace lining up once you are clear and present to truly see. To me it feels like that's the real world: to do what is needed in the moment with a positive mindset and a loving heart. Do what gives you the joy of using your talents, and that which makes you feel you are really meant to do it.

The idea of having to work in a presumably secure job for a fixed salary to live a lifestyle that others live does not work for me. I don't believe in it. It doesn't feel good. And as much as my reasoning and upbringing does not want to fully accept my truth, life has taught me various lessons. Some of the most obvious lessons were burn-out, divorce and cancer. Once I was knocked off my motorcycle and got compensation for loss suffered. Once I got money literally I had forgotten about ... I always had more than I needed.

Today, I fully appreciate that I really don't need to work a mediocre job I am not made for, nor work in a negative environment, just to secure my survival. It's definitely not true for me due to my belief system. On the other hand, I don't have a problem to help out in almost any job if I can, when needed. My energy runs through my system differently than before. Less worrying, less pondering sets free a lot of energy that I can use for other things. I don't do much at all, just living a very simple and humble life. Yet, I do feel rich, living the way I choose, starting most of the mornings practicing yoga, walking, or just watching the beauty of nature. I love the fact that I never know what comes up next. Just like everybody else, I don't know what comes next and being aware of it gives me a special pleasure.

Money has come to me in ways I couldn't even have imagined. Not all positive! But it came. One time I was booked to interpret for a professional meeting in Switzerland. Turns out I was booked by some mobster.

So to sum it up, I figured it is worth learning to consciously choose. I am in the process of learning and practicing. And I don't need much to be happy. A lifestyle swimming in the ocean many days in a year, going for hikes, meeting friends, making friends, listening and learning, exchanging and traveling a bit to me is rich. I still work as a walking coach, if somebody finds me and asks for my help. I still do modeling if I like the job and the story behind the product. Jobs that are in my interest and go with my values. I am still in the process of learning to say no. And in the process of trusting what I feel, taking it seriously and not only saying what I want, but going for it.

Last year, I got back into business trainings. It just happened without having to market my services. Later I decided to be more specific and work only for the people in the industries I support. So I canceled my only well-paid job for a pharmaceutical industry. One door closes, one door opens. It's my choice. How do I choose? It's the conscious effort to put out an intention, let go and trust. It's not hard, not tiring. It is cutting away what doesn't suit me, what doesn't feel right, what doesn't go along with my beliefs and allowing new things to show up. Less distraction. Like a deep-down felt tingling that wants to tell me what is really important for me.

**

Everybody needs to find out their own language to communicate. That's not hard work; in fact, if it becomes hard work it no longer works, it hinders the process of letting go and creating freely. It blocks the connection, there is no more flow, it is like forcing God to fulfill your wish and still doubting it will happen.

21 - What Difference Did the Shamanic Work Make?

In summary, I find it most hilarious that we really can create what we want. The only trick is not to mistake what our ego wants and what you, yourself, or your soul really needs. And at the same time no fighting but make friends with the ego and become more compassionate with yourself. Then, the pearls can line up.

Whenever you hear "yes, but," "if only," "I can't because ... ," etc., that's probably monkey mind chatter stemming from the ego, that thing that doesn't really exist, that is just like a software running the system in the background in some faraway, hidden files. That thing that was originally there to make things easier and to secure survival and then tried to be bigger than ourselves and bigger than God. Instead of trying to kill the survival software or identifying with it, we are better off learning how to use it. Ayahuasca doesn't do that practical part. You have to walk that path for yourself.

22 - From Now On, What?

Living the Lessons

Has life become easier? In a certain way, yes: within the last years I have practiced to apply what I've learned. I couldn't just do it. It was a conscious effort. It was easy in some way, because I got to experience very clearly the difference between feeling, accepting and letting go versus suffering over and over again. Situations I just can't go along with, can only make me suffer, until I choose how to deal with it. Accept it, change it or leave it.

Pain is one thing, suffering another. Fear is one thing, suffering another. Anger is one thing, suffering another. Sadness is one thing, suffering another.

During the last years I had experiences just like any other year before Ayahuasca. And it took only a few months until my alertness to staying present diminished. But it is easy to realize when I lose track, lost connection with myself, got stuck in programs: I find myself in a state of suffering. That's the signal.

Suffering had become the key, the ultimate wake-up call to staying present. Whenever I was suffering, I was judging, my expectations hadn't been met, I felt disconnected, and as a consequence I felt low. It is about allowing myself to feel whatever there is and accept what I feel, instead of fighting it or putting a lot of mental effort and energy into conflict and stressing out. That's suffering. It's more of a mental process. It's the judgment of what is going on. I am still in the process of learning and practicing. Walking in the woods helps. Praying helps.

"Yes, but how can you make sure to do the right thing, if you don't judge into good and bad ..." is what the ongoing voice in the back of the head might say. That is the cat biting itself in the tail: thinking,

22 - From Now On, What?

thinking, thinking, in order to make the right judgment, to then have a good reason to feel low. Instead of just accepting feelings caused by a situation, allowing this feeling to appear and be perceived first. Feel it! Accept the feeling compassionately and then, once back in a state of being okay, deal with the situation in a more relaxed way. Let go of resistance and fighting. Exit the circle of going round and round with thinking.

Every movie has an evolving story. If we cut out episode 2 to 11, we're not even going to understand and enjoy the last episode.

Last year in the summer, again, I felt some kind of a calling to go to back to South America. Both Anthony and I could imagine going to Ecuador for some time, to live a simple life, even simpler than we already live it. Just for the sake of experiencing it. Then, our habitual thinking mind kicked in. We were looking for a good reason to allow that to happen. We needed to sublease the flat to not have double fix costs. Blah blah blah. I started checking flights and locations we might want to visit. We wanted to go in the winter, when it is coldish in Mallorca. It felt like an eternity from summer to the winter. One more time, I had not applied what I had learned. But as soon as I noticed the resistance in my system to the idea of spending another winter here, and waiting however long it will take to finally travel, I remembered: this is a subtle, elegant way of suffering. Stop it! Let go of the attachment!

If I am wishing not to be here but there, visualizing, imagining, planning, preparing, automatically I am less present. And that's what I don't want to do any longer. Not after three months in the Amazon and nineteen healing plant ceremonies. Not after abuse, burnout, divorce, cancer.

Making the very best of a situation does not mean to suppress true feelings or twist reasoning, talking any golden shit.

My job is to distinguish between what is real and what's not. My job is to create by intention. Follow up on feelings. INTUITION. Use gut feelings as guidelines. Not to be confused with emotions from the past that were triggered by somebody pushing our button right now. That's the work! Notice the difference of what is real and what is an old program appearing. Appreciate what is. Living the here and now.

Headless Chicken

Listen to your heart, and don't get stubborn about making this wish happen now, no matter what! Tuning into some kind of flow. Going with nature, not against. Trusting God, not the media. Doing what's just, not what brings me and me only instant pleasure, at the cost of the greater good.

From now on, I choose to listen to my gut feeling, listen to my heart, and recognize when I am getting off track. This track is not an external road or goal. Those external goals in the material world are more of a decoration of the process. The real deal is the energy we are filled with, what we really are. And the clue is to direct that energy. That energy being life or love vibration or creative force itself, creating, the creator and creation that is what we are. We are not just a body of flesh and a computer. We are self-directing, expanding, creative energy. The directive is love.

Unfortunately, I haven't learned from Ayahuasca how to create from the viewpoint of a human being. I only saw how that works from the viewpoint of the soul, individual spiritual energy. That's not satisfying for a thinking mind in a three-dimensional world.

It is like looking into a kaleidoscope from the wrong side, it takes switching perspective to remember what I really am: spiritual energy, love, made by and as a part of God. A spiritual being with a human experience that is embodied, alive here now to use that energy in such a way that resonates with itself (me) and it (the universe) which is inseparably connected anyway. Talking about those things feels like juggling with words. Word is power of creation. I want to learn to use less words, less pollution, less distraction, less confusion. Simplify more. Spend the day going down to the seafront in the morning for some yoga, coming home, have a meal, go out in the woods in the afternoon to get some firewood. Maybe write. Maybe invite friends over for tea. And that can be enough. No more sabotaging emotions caused by thought of not being good enough, not doing enough, not doing the right thing, doubts or mental chatter. Peace.

For me it is all about taking care of your energy. Love. And there is still room to improve. Everything I choose to do that doesn't resonate with love or similar is a mis-use of energy. Gets me off-track. That's about it.

22 - From Now On, What?

So now I am all open for possibilities. Every day I seem to be jumping off a jumping board without knowing where I'm falling. Every day gives me a new opportunity to experience something new, expand, learn, share. What does really matter? Whether my expectations are met or not? What if I just let go of the expectations? And when the mind kicks in saying: hang on a minute, isn't that too simple, too empty, too little complicated? Aren't you here for something more important? Then, I remember to tune into my true being, to get into a kind of trance or meditation state. A practice that allows me to get over compulsive thinking habits, and just be in the moment.

By allowing myself to jump into the unknown day by day again and again, detaching from an outcome, amazing things appear on the horizon. God in action and I may give him my hand and trust. Things that I could not have planned.

Sometimes it takes a long time for some kind of sign to show up and confirm my faith in the process. That's the test. Can I keep my cool? Can I stay positive? Do I trust? Can I let go? Let go of unconscious compulsive wanting-to-control behavior, that doesn't serve me or anybody else. Just like too much Internet, too many movies, too many sweets, coffee, alcohol, etc. The only reason for that unconscious behavior is to distract from feeling important feelings here and now that guide your direction. That's when they refer to "life is what happens while you are busy making other plans." We only want to feel joy, that is our conditioning, even though every other feeling is just as important to be felt and to guide us. Too much or too little of anything leads to an imbalance. Sports and exercise, games and play, study, work, sleep, sex and rock 'n' roll.

"Mother Ayahuasca" didn't talk about measurement. But did get the message that I have a choice. I can choose what feels harmonious and what doesn't. It takes feeling, intuition. I can choose to get drunk, to stay sober, or to drink just little. I can choose black and I can choose white. I'm free to choose. That's why feeling is so important! No feeling, not tuned in, no guidelines, no direction. To me, intuition is the direction. Gut feeling is the street sign at the next crossing in the process of creating.

Boosting the mood with some extra shots, drugs or hypes makes us numb, blurred, unclear. It may be helpful at times.

Headless Chicken

My biggest fear had been fear of negative feelings such as fear itself, anger or sadness. I had not been aware that I had that fear. I had just learned to train my mind in such a way that I wouldn't feel anything at all, numb, in case of "negative" feelings I didn't know how to cope with. But the emotion was not gone, it was just suppressed, messing up the whole process of creating life. And now, I am allowing myself to feel any feelings, what we consider beautiful or terribly scary. It doesn't matter, egal, it just is what it is. Permitting to feel everything honestly and then deciding how to deal with it make me free. Free to choose according to the signals I get. And it only works as long as I remember who or what I am. Identified with the thinking mind and the body, I just repeat yesterday's stories as if I was not really alive at all.

Most astonishingly, the process hasn't become dull, boring or lacked meaning, ever since. I don't lack ideas, and new projects come up that tune in with my intentions and talents. They might be different than expected but fit. All I know is, it seems much more interesting than if I would have planned and lined up the next five years ahead of time by myself. What really counts for me today is how I spend my lifetime in every moment, in what state of being.

All I know is that I don't know a lot. I am okay with not knowing whether I will go to Ecuador, stay there, come back, or do something totally different. I'm okay with not knowing, whether I will have grandchildren someday or not. I am okay with not knowing where the next money is coming from. I am okay that we all, me, my loved ones and all of you will leave the body someday, and quite possibly that might not happen at the same time. I'm okay with letting go of friends, and making new ones. I'm okay with changing my mind. I can live with other people who change their minds. I am okay with letting go, accepting, changing or leaving. I am free to choose how to respond. Ayahuasca ceremonies are over for me. We need no drugs to be connected. And that might change as well. Not as long I stay tuned in, connected with my inner self, I will know what to do and when the time is right for some kind of move. And even though right now I might not have any plan, or what I envisioned just didn't workout, I know I will make the real important decisions at the right time at the right place and I will feel it. I trust. I trust that I am not alone and deep down I know there is a higher force in action, God, who holds the reigns of life and acts according to very specific laws. Failing is

22 - From Now On, What?

okay. HE is forgiving, but it takes me to forgive myself and others as well, regret, ask for forgiveness and learn from it. Better fail than not live at all. Learning by doing is an acceptable approach to life. It takes courage, and it takes to be present, but is much more fun than just copying and repeating yesterday's experiences.

So I keep on walking and accompanying others when somebody comes along asking for my services. Same with acting: if roles that fit my nature, values and intentions show up, great. If not, great too. Plenty good enough. I experiment doing improv theater in Spanish language, for the fun of experiencing the magic of the moment when nobody knows what will happen next and everybody still creates the play in the very moment together. Just like real life.

Open to take on new projects that come our way if it feels right. Maybe will do more business training again, but in an industry worth supporting. When it shows up I will recognize it.

We don't have to limit ourselves to wearing one hat only. We can. We need no batches or boxes to fit into. We are energy. Vivid. The process of walking the path is already what we call life. Getting a taste of the paradox of intending, letting go and enjoying the path, even when it rains. Acknowledging and appreciating tears and fears. Then, sometimes crying out loud, or laughing out loud, daring to share my bit of vibration to the universe.

There's a lot of people here in Europe offering Ayahuasca ceremonies now. It became a real hype. Almost everybody seems to think this is something you have to do nowadays. Like a new hip drug, a new hip spiritual thing, a new ecstasy. I would be very careful where and with whom I do that. Whether you should do this at all and with a Western shaman or somebody who has been doing this in the third generation in the Amazon rain forest you've got to ask your guts and pay the consequences!

It doesn't matter, how much time you have, or how much money. Everything will fall into place, when the time is right. And then there won't be any doubt. Our journey here works with or without tripping. It takes our our body, our mind, our awareness, our love. Get ready for it! Trust!

Headless Chicken

I believe that the knowledge and healing power of "Mother Ayahuasca" is with everybody all the time. We are nature. We are vibration. Connecting with that healing power is connecting with parts of ourselves. If your motivation is to check out Ayahuasca, see some cool pictures or out of curiosity experience what your buddies experienced, don't be surprised if that was the wrong choice. I believe it can be dangerous. There are negative energies out there that can mess a human mind up for the rest of their life. Ayahuasca is not any safer in the jungle than anywhere else. Iquitos has become a Mecca for want-to-be shamans with their lucrative Ayahuasca businesses. Sexual abuse was reported where shamans had sex with their "patients" on drugs without their consent.

Reason and statistics are not a good way to base a decision on. Trust yourself, your inner voice, your intuition.

Ayahuasca didn't give any answers, but temporarily took away filters, to reveal what was hidden away by protective ego mechanisms. Knowing and wanting to know alone is not helpful at all. It takes your own love and compassion to heal. Nothing comes from outside, even if you had a glimpse into the spirit world. How you vibrate here and now is what counts, not just what you know: positive or negative, loving or fearful, believing or doubting, narrow-minded, mean-spirited, stubborn or understanding, compassionate and solution oriented. You have free choice to make up your own heart and mind in every moment, no Ayahuasca, therapist or priest has the right to do that for you. If anything, the rather dangerous hard-core experience confirmed what is written in the Bible and revealed in meditation: Bring our own mind and heart together in order to make the right decisions.

* * *

Ayahuasca has given me a confirmation about something I already knew deep down inside, but I just didn't dare to trust it. Now, every day I witness some kind of magic, connectedness, creativity, healing power, intelligence behind everything. And if I listen, I am—part of it. Now, I trust nature. I trust God. Sometimes I still forget and get stuck again. And then I reconnect, go into the woods, pray and remember. No Ayahuasca needed.

God never sleeps.

Epilogue

Kosho Uchiyama wrote in *Opening the Hand of Thought*: "When we look up we tend to think that clouds mount up high in the sky, but I read, that if we draw an eight-inch circle to represent the earth, the pencil line is the thickness of the entire atmosphere. The clouds are just things flowing here and there, appearing and disappearing within that thin space."

* * *

To tell personal stories honestly and openly the way you experienced them at the time is a way to become more understanding and compassionate with yourself. Once you can look at it from a distance, you see the bigger picture beyond the clouds. It makes more sense. It helps you better understand that paradox of self, that individual living being, that strives for a "pseudo-elegant lifestyle" and that is also a part of the one, yearning to live the truth here and now, as one living energy.

* * *

Silence is the key to connect to that innermost part of ourselves. It is silence. The space beyond the monkey mind is where everything starts, is and ends. Ayahuasca helps temporarily to tame the monkey mind. So you can see. But it doesn't last. And it doesn't help you to remember. Many people go back again and again, because they forgot. We need silent time regularly to connect with that space where we face the truth. It is there, where we can remember.

In silence we find the answer to our most profound questions. That's where we remember who we are and what we are here for.

Expressing oneself fearlessly is sharing oneself and connecting. You are here to be yourself and to share yourself with or without a name tag with a title. Don't follow like sheep any longer! Question, feel what feels right. And dare to share! I am about to learn it!

In that sense, explore yourself in silence, find your throne inside and go out and share yourself with the world!

LOVE!

yaduma@me.com
http://theWalkingGuru.org

About the Author

Something just didn't work out. And it wasn't just the environment, it was the way she faced life situations, her attitude, her judging, her fears, her habits, her conditioning. That was Manuela's lesson in 2000, when she experienced malign melanoma, advanced skin cancer, right after burn-out and divorce, leaving marriage, job and "security" behind. She had to be re-operated right away. Next week might be too late. This is when she realized, that she didn't care about her life, it felt rather like a struggle and a burden. But dying was not an option: she was mother of two small children. This is when things started changing. She hadn't appreciated her own life but tried to do the right thing, had been hard on herself with a lack of compassion for her own needs and priorities. She decided to experiment a total "reset", learn how to change her own attitude and inner mechanisms. After trainings in Mental Power, Coaching, Yoga and Hypnosis and regular personal retreats, she developed an innovative new way of supporting people to change habits that included mind, body and soul. Her Yaduma program was prize-awarded in 2006.

The message: if we stop searching for answers out there and dare to explore inside who we are and why we are here, we can find not only the key to meaning, mission and happiness but the kind of relationship to ourselves, God and the world that we most desire.

Other Books by Ozark Mountain Publishing, Inc.

Dolores Cannon
A Soul Remembers Hiroshima
Between Death and Life
Conversations with Nostradamus,
  Volume I, II, III
The Convoluted Universe -Book One,
  Two, Three, Four, Five
The Custodians
Five Lives Remembered
Jesus and the Essenes
Keepers of the Garden
Legacy from the Stars
The Legend of Starcrash
The Search for Hidden Sacred Knowledge
They Walked with Jesus
The Three Waves of Volunteers and the
  New Earth
Aron Abrahamsen
Holiday in Heaven
Out of the Archives – Earth Changes
Justine Alessi & M. E. McMillan
Rebirth of the Oracle
Kathryn/Patrick Andries
Naked in Public
Kathryn Andries
The Big Desire
Dream Doctor
Soul Choices: Six Paths to Find Your Life
  Purpose
Soul Choices: Six Paths to Fulfilling
  Relationships
Patrick Andries
Owners Manual for the Mind
Dan Bird
Finding Your Way in the Spiritual Age
Waking Up in the Spiritual Age
Julia Cannon
Soul Speak – The Language of Your Body
Ronald Chapman
Seeing True
Albert Cheung
The Emperor's Stargate
Jack Churchward
Lifting the Veil on the Lost Continent of
  Mu
The Stone Tablets of Mu
Sherri Cortland
Guide Group Fridays
Raising Our Vibrations for the New Age

Spiritual Tool Box
Windows of Opportunity
Patrick De Haan
The Alien Handbook
Paulinne Delcour-Min
Spiritual Gold
Michael Dennis
Morning Coffee with God
God's Many Mansions
Carolyn Greer Daly
Opening to Fullness of Spirit
Anita Holmes
Twidders
Aaron Hoopes
Reconnecting to the Earth
Victoria Hunt
Kiss the Wind
Patricia Irvine
In Light and In Shade
Kevin Killen
Ghosts and Me
Diane Lewis
From Psychic to Soul
Donna Lynn
From Fear to Love
Maureen McGill
Baby It's You
Maureen McGill & Nola Davis
Live from the Other Side
Curt Melliger
Heaven Here on Earth
Henry Michaelson
And Jesus Said – A Conversation
Dennis Milner
Kosmos
Andy Myers
Not Your Average Angel Book
Guy Needler
Avoiding Karma
Beyond the Source – Book 1, Book 2
The Anne Dialogues
The Curators
The History of God
The Origin Speaks
James Nussbaumer
And Then I Knew My Abundance
The Master of Everything
Mastering Your Own Spiritual Freedom

For more information about any of the above titles, soon to be released titles,
or other items in our catalog, write, phone or visit our website:
PO Box 754, Huntsville, AR 72740
479-738-2348/800-935-0045
www.ozarkmt.com

Other Books by Ozark Mountain Publishing, Inc.

Sherry O'Brian
Peaks and Valleys
Riet Okken
The Liberating Power of Emotions
Gabrielle Orr
Akashic Records: One True Love
Let Miracles Happen
Victor Parachin
Sit a Bit
Nikki Pattillo
A Spiritual Evolution
Children of the Stars
Rev. Grant H. Pealer
A Funny Thing Happened on the
   Way to Heaven
Worlds Beyond Death
Victoria Pendragon
Born Healers
Feng Shui from the Inside, Out
Sleep Magic
The Sleeping Phoenix
Michael Perlin
Fantastic Adventures in Metaphysics
Walter Pullen
Evolution of the Spirit
Debra Rayburn
Let's Get Natural with Herbs
Charmian Redwood
A New Earth Rising
Coming Home to Lemuria
David Rivinus
Always Dreaming
Richard Rowe
Imagining the Unimaginable
M. Don Schorn
Elder Gods of Antiquity
Legacy of the Elder Gods
Gardens of the Elder Gods
Reincarnation...Stepping Stones of Life
Garnet Schulhauser
Dance of Eternal Rapture
Dance of Heavenly Bliss

Dancing Forever with Spirit
Dancing on a Stamp
Manuella Stoerzer
Headless Chicken
Annie Stillwater Gray
Education of a Guardian Angel
The Dawn Book
Work of a Guardian Angel
Blair Styra
Don't Change the Channel
Who Catharted
Natalie Sudman
Application of Impossible Things
L.R. Sumpter
Judy's Story
The Old is New
We Are the Creators
Jim Thomas
Tales from the Trance
Nicholas Vesey
Living the Life-Force
Janie Wells
Embracing the Human Journey
Payment for Passage
Dennis Wheatley/ Maria Wheatley
The Essential Dowsing Guide
Maria Wheatley
Druidic Soul Star Astrology
Jacquelyn Wiersma
The Zodiac Recipe
Sherry Wilde
The Forgotten Promise
Lyn Willmoth
A Small Book of Comfort
Stuart Wilson & Joanna Prentis
Atlantis and the New Consciousness
Beyond Limitations
The Essenes -Children of the Light
The Magdalene Version
Power of the Magdalene
Robert Winterhalter
The Healing Christ

For more information about any of the above titles, soon to be released titles,
or other items in our catalog, write, phone or visit our website:
PO Box 754, Huntsville, AR 72740
479-738-2348/800-935-0045
www.ozarkmt.com